GOOD MORNING – IT'S MARGARET

CH00600942

The Reverend Marga
but has lived in the nor
Since 1973 sh
St James' Church
and was or
She is also Broadcasting Officer for the diocese of York,
Anglican Adviser to Yorkshire Television,
and broadcasts frequently both locally
and nationally.
She is a regular contributor to BBC Radio 2's
Pause for Thought, and to the
British Forces Broadcasting Service's religious programmes.

Good Morning – it's Margaret

MARGARET CUNDIFF

TRiANGle

First published 1988
Triangle/SPCK
Holy Trinity Church
Marylebone Road
London NW1 4DU

British Library Cataloguing in Publication Data

Cundiff, Margaret
  Good morning – it's Margaret.
  1. Devotional literature
  I. Title
  242   BV4832.2

  ISBN 0–281–04332–9

Typeset by Inforum Ltd, Portsmouth
Printed in Great Britain by
Hazell Watson & Viney Limited
Member of BPCC plc
Aylesbury Bucks

For

Derek Jameson, for allowing me to share 'the great
British public' with him on Radio 2's
Pause for Thought

Ted King of the British Forces Broadcasting
Service,
who sends me around the world 'on air'

and all my many friends in local radio,
both BBC and Independent Local Radio.

Thank you for the fun, the friendship and the
air time.

Acknowledgements

The greater part of this book is based on talks first broadcast on BBC Radio 2, on *Pause for Thought*, as part of the Derek Jameson programme on Thursday mornings.

'God's Top Ten' was first broadcast on Radio Aire.

The 'Meditation on the Lord's Prayer' was written for BBC Ceefax.

The following are based on broadcasts for the British Forces Broadcasting Service: 'Shopping around'; 'Judge not'; 'Why worry?'; 'Never too late'; 'Plastic money can kill'; 'Sunday is special'; 'Hands up!'; 'Right on time'.

Bible quotations are from the *Good News Bible*, copyright © American Bible Society, 1966, 1971, 1976, published by the Bible Society/Collins, and are used by permission.

Contents

Preface

One of the questions I am frequently asked is, 'What size is your congregation?' My tongue-in-cheek reply – because I don't believe in playing the numbers game anyway – is 'About a hundred on Sundays and several million on Thursdays.'

I am a parish deacon. Each week I preach sermons from the pulpit, in my home church of St James, Selby, or in one of the many and varied churches I am invited to in the Diocese of York and beyond. As a regular contributor to *Pause for Thought* on BBC Radio 2 and similar programmes on local radio, as well as the British Forces Broadcasting Service which is heard world-wide, I speak to the millions, most of whom I have never met, and never will, except through radio. I try not to preach at them – after all, they are not a congregation, but listeners; and although only a very brave person in church might get up and walk out during a sermon, a listener can remove me in a moment, by turning me off!

A hundred – a million. No. I am not speaking to 'them', but to you, a friend – my friend, because that is how I see you. You whom I meet on air, I just enjoy sitting down and sharing with you my thoughts and ideas, my faith, and the fun I have in life. I try to be honest with you, so sometimes I may sound rather serious, even a little fearful, doubtful, or occasionally annoyed – but that's me!

So many people have written to me and asked for copies of my scripts, and I have been glad to send them a copy. Others have said, 'Please put them in a book.' So here we are – a selection of my 'thoughts', first given on the BBC and

BFBS, to which I have added appropriate verses of Scripture and a short prayer.

Congregation – listeners – readers – no, friends! My friends – thank you for giving me the privilege of sharing with you.

Margaret Cundiff
St James' Day
July 25th, 1987

Be happy

I went into the local newsagent's to buy a couple of cards – one for a friend's birthday and another to congratulate a couple on their wedding anniversary – and I had a good browse through the selection on offer. There were, as the notice said, 'Cards for every occasion', from passing exams to moving house, from the sentimental, 'hearts and flowers' types to the comic – and sometimes quite rude! But all of them were saying basically the same thing: 'We wish you happiness' – Happy Birthday; Happy Anniversary; Congratulations on a Happy Event.

We do want people to be happy, to get the most out of life and to enjoy themselves. And what is more, we want to be happy ourselves. But ought we to look for our own happiness? Is it right to pursue happiness? Isn't that rather selfish?

The American Declaration of Independence says this: 'We hold these truths to be self-evident. That all men are created equal, that they are endowed by their Creator with certain inalienable rights. That among these are life, liberty and the pursuit of happiness.' And St Thomas Aquinas said: 'Lust and pride are the roots and sprouts of vice, as the desire for happiness is the root of all virtue.' So maybe we should take the subject of happiness far more seriously than we do, not leaving it to chance, or hit-and-miss, but setting out to be happy – aiming for that quite deliberately.

Are you happy? Do you think it is possible to be really happy – especially in the world we live in today, with all its sadness and grief, its violence and unfairness? I ask myself these questions, and I must say I am happy – most of the time. And so I should be. I have a loving family, a very satisfying job, I live in a pleasant part of Yorkshire, I have very tolerant friends and I enjoy good health. Yet I know people who have none of these things and are still happy; there is something about them that is quite irresistible. And I know others who have everything going for them, materially speaking, yet they are absolute miseries.

So happiness doesn't depend on material things, or on circumstances, or even on other people; it is something more than all these. I go back to St Thomas Aquinas for the clue, for he also said: 'There can be no complete and final happiness for us, save in the vision of God.'

True happiness is to be found in God, in our seeking after him. And if we want to be happy, then we only begin to discover it when we discover God – when we get tuned in to him, and begin to realise his love for us.

But how do we get tuned in? We have first got to be switched on, and on the right channel.

I find that this happens for me through prayer, when I make a space in my life to be quiet in God's presence. It may sometimes be within a public act of worship in church – the fact that others around me are doing the same thing can be an enormous help. It can be in the quiet of an empty church building. But it can also be when I'm walking down the road, sitting on top of a bus, or driving into town; doing the washing up, or resting with my feet up after a hard day. The place doesn't matter; the desire does.

We sometimes make the mistake of thinking that prayer, and meditation and contemplation, are only for special people – 'professional Christians' like priests and vicars, monks and nuns. But prayer is for everybody, and anybody. It is a matter of letting go – and just enjoying God's presence. And as we feel the warmth of his presence, as we come into that freedom of 'just being', then we are able to release all that is making us unhappy – the problems, the anxieties, the people – and in exchange to know healing, peace, and that elusive thing . . . happiness.

It all sounds so simple, doesn't it? Maybe too simple. And yet most big questions have very simple answers – if we will allow ourselves to see them.

You will show me the path that leads to life;
your presence fills me with joy
and brings me pleasure for ever.

Psalm 16.11

Thank you, Lord, for the joy of knowing you;
that I can come straight into your presence,
and tell you everything.
Thank you for being you, my Lord, my God, my all, my happiness.

Plain speaking

'A rose by any other name would smell as sweet.' I'm sure Shakespeare's Juliet was quite right. But which would you prefer to have in your garden, a rose called Fragrant Cloud, or one called Fogbound? Would you book bed and breakfast at Gasworks View when for the same price you could stay at Honeysuckle Cottage? I knew a girl who insisted that her husband-to-be changed his name by deed poll before she would marry him. She just couldn't face being Mrs Buggins for the rest of her life.

I was sitting next to a man the other day who had about four days' growth of beard. I asked him, 'Is that beard coming or going?' 'Neither,' he said. 'It's supposed to look like this. It's called designer stubble.' Well, I thought he was pulling my leg, so when my son came home I asked him, 'Is there such a thing as designer stubble?'. 'Oh yes,' he said. 'What does it look like?' I persisted. 'Like I did when I came back from my fishing trip and hadn't bothered to shave all week,' was his matter-of-fact reply.

So, designer stubble it is – I'm convinced now. It sounds quite attractive, doesn't it? Almost virtuous. A bit like when a badly behaved child starts throwing things and his mother says, 'He's so creative?'; or that vicious little dog goes for your ankle, and the owner stands there smiling without doing anything to help, and says, 'He's just playful'. Or when the sullen are 'pensive', or the downright rude 'outspoken'.

Every advertiser knows that the name given to a product is of vital importance; it can make it or break it. That is why they go to such trouble to get exactly the right name, something that will convey a particular image in the mind of

4

the consumer. Just think about some of the names given to the popular makes of cars, chocolates or perfumes.

Yet, give something a fancy name, and you can get away with – I almost said murder. And it is true, murder gets dressed up in very respectable language – like 'unfortunate incident', 'reprisal', 'victim of circumstances'. We don't cheat any more, we are 'astute'. We never tell lies, we are 'diplomatic'. And if we have a 'meaningful relationship' with someone else's husband or wife, that's not adultery – is it? Remember that old fashioned expression 'living in sin'? No one does that any more; it's called a 'current live-in arrangement' – because we must never use the word sin. Mistake, yes. Error of judgement, maybe. But sin, never. I can call myself indiscreet, ill-advised, impetuous, or even weak-willed; that makes me feel much better.

But the trouble is that the Bible calls a spade a spade, or rather a sin a sin; and even the most modern translations have not found a word to replace that nasty-sounding three-letter word. In fact, the Bible uses it over and over again, and sadly it seems to describe many things in my own life.

Of course, I could say that I never commit any sins, and find a gentler, nicer way of expressing my – er – errors of judgement. But St John spelled it out like this: 'If we say we have no sin, we deceive ourselves, and the truth is not in us.' Plain speaking that! But maybe it's the best way. I know where I stand then, don't I?

Be merciful to me, O God,
  because of your constant love.
Because of your great mercy
  wipe away my sins!
Wash away all my evil
  and make me clean from my sin!

I recognise my faults;
  I am always conscious of my sins.
I have sinned against you
  And done what you consider evil.

Psalm 51.1–4

Lord, hear my prayer,
and let my cry come to you. Amen.

Shopping around

The thing that annoys me about supermarkets is that I can get round quickly, gather into my trolley everything I need, from stewing steak to sewing needles, from frozen chicken to car polish – and then get stuck at the check-out. It's like Russian roulette, gambling on which check-out to stand at, and I nearly always seem to back a loser – 'This till is closing now, luv,' or the person in front of me starts to argue about the price of baked beans.

The other day I was standing waiting patiently, or not so patiently, in the queue, and for want of anything better to do I was watching my fellow customers. They all seemed to think they were in the Grand Prix, racing round like there was no tomorrow, hurling things into the trolleys and making a mad dash for the check-out. As soon as they – and me included – got through the check-out, it was a race to the car, open the boot, shove it all in, and away. It all seems so impersonal, with no one talking to anyone, just intent on filling up those trolleys and getting away before anyone speaks.

Supermarkets may have put a great deal more choice on the shelves for us, but they have taken the heart out of shopping. The old corner shops, and the family grocers who knew everyone with their likes and dislikes, didn't just sell goods. They were father confessors, garden experts, problem solvers, DIY advisers, information offices, lost property departments, and in some cases marriage brokers. Shopping was a social affair; people talked to each other, and had time to listen and to help. It was a communal activity, rather than this impersonal private trolley-push.

Thank goodness there are still some corner shops left, and old-fashioned shopkeepers. I suppose it is quicker in the long run at the supermarket, but what do we do with the time we save?

Perhaps I shouldn't blame the supermarket, but blame myself. If I bothered to stop and chat, smile at people, tickle the baby who is yelling his head off, then maybe I could do a bit of good, for myself as well as for other people.

Jesus always had time for people. Even when he was tired out and sat down by a well in the hot sun, he had time to talk to a woman who wanted to have an argument. He had time to go and have a meal with a dishonest tax collector, and show him a new way of life. He had time, even when he was dying on the cross, to comfort the man beside him and give him hope. He always had time for people, because he cared about them. He didn't blame the system; he took time.

So I've resolved to take it a bit more slowly round the supermarket, to look at people, not just at things on shelves. And if I do get stuck in the queue, then I can talk to my neighbour who is waiting beside me. It could be the start of a 'put people back into shopping' campaign. That's a personal service we could all give, couldn't we?

Your speech should always be pleasant and interesting, and you should know how to give the right answer to everyone. Colossians 4.6

Time, Lord, is your gift to me, and you want me to enjoy it, share it and reverence it. Today I will meet people who no one has time for; help me to give freely of your gift of time to them, as an offering of thanksgiving and love. For Christ's sake.

This above all

I've still got the autograph book I had as a youngster. It says in the front: 'This book belongs to Margaret Smith, aged 12'. I enjoy going through it from time to time. I've not got many celebrities in it – mainly my school friends, teachers and relatives. There is all the usual sort of stuff like: 'By hook or by crook, I'll be last in this book', and

> 2Ys U R
> 2Ys U B
> I C U R
> 2Ys 4 Me

One of my teachers wrote the quotation:

> *This above all, to thine own self be true,*
> *And it must follow as the night the day*
> *Thou canst not then be false to any man.*

The words are by William Shakespeare, so the English teacher said, and I'm sure she was right. English was never my strong point!

I never really got on with the teacher who wrote those words, but as I have got older, and from time to time re-read what she wrote in my book, I have been very thankful for them.

'To thine own self be true.' I was reminded of this by some controversial comments by the Chief Constable of Manchester, James Anderton. There is a man who is true to himself – whatever you may think of him, you can't deny that. He has come in for a great deal of criticism for his outspoken statements. People think it is not quite the thing for Chief

Constables to speak out in the name of God. They are not paid for that, they are paid to run a police force. They should leave speaking out for God to Archbishops and Cardinals or perhaps the local vicar, the Salvation Army, and that sort of professional religious body.

And yet, why shouldn't a Chief Constable express his faith in God, his love for Jesus Christ and his belief in the Bible? If he was a football fanatic, his enthusiasm would be applauded. If he was an expert on antique furniture, for instance, he would be invited here, there and everywhere to speak about his hobby, and to encourage others to discover the joys of antiques. He'd be a favourite on the chat shows, and everyone would say, 'What a nice man. It's good he has got such an interesting hobby.'

Yet because his 'thing' is his Christian faith, because he is an enthusiast for God, he is labelled as a crank, and doubts are expressed about the state of his mind, whether he is fit to run a police force. And from some quarters come shouts of, 'Keep quiet, or resign.'

Well, I am a Christian, and lots of other things besides, but I hope my faith comes into every bit of my life – as a wife and mother, a friend and colleague, in the village where I live, in the letters I write, and the conversations I have, with individuals or groups. I know I am a Christian minister and expected to say religious things, but I don't put my faith on with my cassock or take it off when I leave church. I am Margaret, a Christian, twenty-four hours a day – because a Christian is someone who knows and loves Jesus Christ – and to be true to myself, to be true to my faith, I've got to express it . . . And so has James Anderton. You may or may not agree with him; that's your privilege. But this is a free country still, I hope, and he is free, or should be, to express his faith.

Jesus said that we are to 'render to Caesar the things that are Caesar's, and to God the things that are God's'. We must all be responsible citizens and pull our weight. But in the end, we have to give an account of our lives to God. So it is a matter of getting our priorities right, isn't it?

I have to be true to myself, James Anderton has to be true to himself, and you have to be true to what you are – honest and straightforward, and open to what others have to say.

For me, I find the best way is to listen to what God has to say; and yes, I talk to him too – and there's nothing strange in that. I am just one of millions who find that prayer – which is what talking to God is – works.

Try it.

The Lord came and stood there, and called as he had before, 'Samuel! Samuel!' Samuel answered, 'Speak; your servant is listening.'

1 Samuel 3.10

Speak, Lord, your servant is listening. Show me the way to go, give me the words to speak, enable me to do your will, whatever it costs. May I be true to you and to myself, this and every day. Amen.

Say No

Our church of St James, Selby, is 120 years old. Now I know that is nothing special when you think of all the really old churches there are around, especially in Yorkshire. But when St James' had its Diamond Jubilee in 1927, it was enjoying a real revival; it was a very exciting time in its history. So we thought, well, 120 years is a Double Diamond, and you know what they say about a Double Diamond – it 'works wonders'. So we embarked on a year of celebration, praying it would work wonders for us all.

We began the celebrations by looking back to the year of our foundation, 1867, and had a Victorian Weekend. The costumes were marvellous; it was amazing what people found in their attics, borrowed or transformed. On the Saturday night we had a Victorian evening round the piano, singing old hymns and songs and listening to dramatic recitations. It was great fun. A friend and I sang a couple of duets: 'When the roll is called up yonder', and a song called, 'Have courage, my boy, to say No'. We had some hilarious rehearsals, and wondered how on earth they used to sing such songs and keep a straight face. But then we suddenly realised just how up to date it was. It goes like this:

> *You're starting, my boy, on life's journey,*
> *Along the great highway of life.*
> *You'll meet with a thousand temptations;*
> *Each city with evil is rife.*
> *The world is a stage of excitement,*
> *There's danger wherever you go.*
> *But if you are tempted in weakness,*
> *Have courage, my boy, to say No.*

And so it goes on, for several verses, in the same vein, ending:

With firmness, with patience and kindness,
Have courage, my boy, to say No.

Now you may be thinking that the words, or some of them, are familiar. I'll give you a clue – Grange Hill. Their anti-drug campaign has the slogan – 'Just say No'. The Victorian sentiment and the modern advice to youngsters are the same – 'Say No'. Not just to drink, drugs or casual sex, but to drifting along with the crowd and letting your standards sink to the lowest common denominator . . . And it's not just youngsters who are faced with temptation, it is all of us.

Can you put your hand on your heart and say you have never succumbed to the temptation of, say, gossiping? Nipping out of work early? Using the firm's materials? Forgetting to return something you've borrowed? Telling lies to get yourself out of a jam? Cooking your expense account? Oh, yes, I know everybody does it, but that doesn't make it right.

I can't blame anyone else for my sins, and neither can you. The answer is quite plain. Whether you use the Grange Hill version or the Victorian one, 'Have courage, my boy (or girl), to say NO'.

Of course, your friends or mates might think you are a sissy, they might drop you, or take the Mickey out of you. But if they do, they're not much use as friends, or mates, are they? And – who knows? – if you have the courage to say No, they might find the courage to say No as well.

So put on God's armour now! Then when the evil day comes, you will be able to resist the enemy's attacks; and after fighting to the end, you will still hold your ground.   Ephesians 6.13

Lord, give me the courage to resist temptation, to be willing even to look a fool or a coward. Give me the strength to say No, and mean it, and give me a willingness to reach out to help others who have succumbed to temptation. For Jesus Christ's sake. Amen.

How old are you?

I often find the advertisements in the newspapers more interesting and thought-provoking than the actual news and features. There is a great art in advertising. It is a bit like fishing. You bait the line with something that appeals to your readers, and then they are hooked and landed – it's the same technique.

So the other day I was flicking through the pages, half exchanging my little car for something more up-market, almost deciding to send off for a winter woolly, and fill in a coupon for details on how to reorganise my kitchen, when some words leaped out at me: '*After sixty, will you be entering old age or a new age?*'

Well, I've a few years to go before I'm sixty, but it made me think of some of the over-sixties I know. There are some who jet around the world, chasing the sun. Others are up to their ears in social work and church activities. There are the ones who give me so much pleasure, like my own parents, well into their seventies but full of life and interest. And in my own church of St James' Selby, it's mostly the golden oldies – if I dare call them that – who have the get-up-and-go attitude; and I can't help thinking of one ninety-year-old who is the life and soul of every party.

But it is not just the hale and hearty, those able to get around the world, or even around the town. Many have neither the cash nor the physical strength to go beyond their own doorstep, but they are some of the most delightful, well-informed and humorous folk I know – they are a tonic to visit.

Then there are the famous over-sixties. Our own Queen has passed that mark now, and just look at the Queen

Mother! Only recently I was listening to the violinist Campoli on his eightieth birthday. Just think of some favourite household names, those who have sharp brains, sparkle, and good sense – writers, actors, artists, entertainers – and I guarantee a good proportion of them are over sixty.

So what is it that separates the old from the young? It's not years, cash, brains or fame. Funnily enough, the advert that set me thinking contained the answer. It said that to live – really live – you need to have a goal, an ambition, a dream, and to go for it.

That is the secret, isn't it? I know, myself, that if I didn't have a goal to aim at, then life could be terribly grey and uninteresting at times, and quite honestly a bit of a bore. But a dream? No, I need more than a dream. I want security. I want to know what's at the end of the line for me – my destiny.

I discovered it many years ago, as a teenager, when I put my faith in Jesus Christ and decided to follow him – not as someone out of a book, or as a moral example, but as a person, a friend, a Saviour. An old-fashioned word, that, but it describes what he is. That was getting on for forty years ago now, but he is still my friend and Saviour. He provides all the incentive I need. He's my future, too.

You have to work out what you want out of life, where you are going – and get after it. Otherwise you could be old long before you are sixty. You could miss out on that new age that should be yours.

For me, I've found what I need in my faith. For you, it might seem to be something entirely different; you may consider you have found *the* answer. All I can say is that I am more than satisfied with Jesus.

It is the spirit of Almighty God
 that comes to men and gives them wisdom.

It is not growing old that makes men wise
  or helps them to know what is right.

Job 32.9

Thank you, Lord, that we are never too young or too old to start a new life. Thank you that it does not come to a dead end, but goes on forever in glorious eternity with you. Amen.

Peace in our time,
O Lord?

On Remembrance Sunday morning the oldest parishioner in our church laid the wreath on the war memorial. He's ninety, and served in the army during the 1914–18 war. His mind is as clear as a bell, and I never get tired of hearing him recount his time as a young Yorkshire lad in the war, because he amazes me with his attitude to life, even though he served through some of the bloodiest battles in history. For Walter Fenton had a simple, direct faith in God, even in the trenches, and he still has that faith more than seventy years on. He has told me many a time of how he prayed during the battles. He prayed, 'Oh, God, get me out of here!' He prayed that he would see his mother again. And he prayed that he wouldn't have to kill anyone.

He described to me the other day how he saw the wounded coming in after a big battle, British and German soldiers helping each other along. One young German soldier dropped his cap, and Walter picked it up and held it out to him. The German said, 'You keep it for a souvenir.' Walter told me, 'I looked at him and thought, What's he done wrong to me? Why should I kill him? He's a nice chap.'

It was perhaps a good thing young Walter kept his thoughts to himself in those days in the trenches. Feeling sorry for German soldiers, not wanting to have anyone's death on his conscience, wouldn't have made him too popular. He wasn't there to think or to pray, but to fight.

I'm so glad Walter survived to tell me his story, though; for so often war is glorified, made out to be admirable, almost a game, like small boys playing with toy soldiers – 'Bang, bang,

18

you're dead!' But war is not a game. And there are no prizes for the winners, for there are no real winners in a war.

Is there such a thing as a just war? I don't know. But war is futile, it is costly, it is a waste. You remember the song 'Where have all the flowers gone?', and the words:

> *When will they ever learn?*
> *When will they ever learn?*

But we don't learn, do we? That is the trouble. And so generation after generation goes on paying the price of war in human grief and tragedy. Walter remembers his young friends and his young enemies, boys of his own age. 'All nice sort of chaps,' he says.

There are not many Walters left now to remember the nice young chaps of the 1914–18 war, or what it was like. But there are plenty who remember and suffer because of the war forty-odd years ago – and only a few years ago in the Falklands. Plenty of nice young chaps, who have mums and wives and children and friends, who never had the chance to live a full life.

On Remembrance Sunday we think about wars and their cost. We have our parades and ceremonies, and then it is all put away for another year, just like putting away the toy soldiers in their boxes, until we feel like playing with them again.

I wouldn't call myself a pacifist. How do I know what I would do if there came another war? I pray that I won't have to face that decision, because if there is another war it will be more terrible than anything recorded so far in the pages of history or in man's memory. My prayer on Remembrance Sunday is: 'Give peace in our time, O Lord, and make me an instrument of your peace.' And I don't put the prayer away after the parades are over. I need to use it every day – and so do you.

How wonderful it is to see
   a messenger coming across the mountains,
   bringing good news, the news of peace!   Isaiah 52.7

'Happy are those who work for peace;
   God will call them his children!'   Matthew 5.9

In the bleak midwinter

Whenever we have a few days of severe weather, we British enjoy recounting our own particular horror stories of the experiences we had in past years, when 'it was even worse than this'. My favourite snow story is of January 1963, when with the weather at its worst I gave birth to our son, and the heating, lighting and water supply at the hospital packed up. My husband Peter tops my story by his account of his hair-raising journey through the blizzard to see his new-born son – and me. His was the last car allowed to go through before the road was closed. Julian now wears a slightly glazed expression as we remind him every birthday of our heroic actions on his behalf. You can't blame him really, since he is now twenty-five!

It seems that adversity, be it caused by the weather, by war, or by any sort of danger or disaster, brings out the best in people. Yes, I know it can also bring out the worst in some, like the shopkeepers or tradesmen who upped their prices when they knew people were desperate for goods or services; but in the main, when there is an emergency, people rise to it.

Maybe we need to experience these things to jog us out of our self-sufficiency. For when life goes along smoothly and predictably, when we are coping nicely and everything in the garden is lovely, we tend to get selfish. We lose ourselves in our own little world, cushioned by our self-made security – then, whoosh! Something critical happens, and we wake up to the fact that there are other people around, and that we need them and they need us.

Those oft-quoted words of John Donne – he wrote them nearly four hundred years ago, but they are right up to date:

'No man is an island, entire of itself. Every man is a piece of the continent, a part of the main . . .' True, isn't it? I know I was so grateful in the last severe winter, when the temperature dropped below zero, that I could turn up the heating, cook warming meals, get up-to-date news of what was happening; and all because so many people were working hard to make sure that the electricity supplies were maintained. The milkman, the paper lad and the postman all struggled up the path with deliveries, the council workmen cleared the roads, and even though I had quite a wait for a train, the waiting room at Selby station was lovely and warm, and there was a very pleasant man to chat to, which made the time fly by . . .

Maybe I imagined it, but I thought people were much nicer during that spell of terrible weather. They smiled more, were more helpful and appreciative of what was being done. The newspapers, radio and television took pleasure in recording good news of neighbourliness or bravery, simple acts of kindness and good humour. Maybe those examples nudged us all into trying a bit harder, checking on our elderly or sick neighbours, giving a hand with shovelling the snow, plodding along to the shops for those who could not get out.

'Love your neighbour as you love yourself,' says Jesus. I reckon a lot of folk did just that during the snowy weather, and found it worked. Well, love always does, doesn't it? It makes the world go round, oils the wheels, smooths out the bumps. It is a pity we don't remember Jesus' words every day, and follow them. It would make life better all round, and not just for a few days in January, or in an emergency.

You will be doing the right thing if you obey the law of the Kingdom, which is found in the scripture, 'Love your neighbour as you love yourself.'
James 2.8

Thank you, Lord, for all those people who help me. Many of them are strangers, and yet they see my need and stretch out a hand to help; they treat me as a friend.

I see so many who need a little help. Often I could help, but I turn away; I'm too busy. When I am tempted to do that, remind me afresh of those who have helped me, who have called me friend, and give me grace to be a friend to others. Amen.

Who was to blame?

We piled on to the early train from York to King's Cross – by 'we', I mean a group of business men complete with brief cases, and me. The carriage was empty except for three young men in jeans and sweaters listening to their cassette radio. I must admit that as I sat down I thought to myself, I hope we are not going to have that noise all the way to London.

Then a voice, a very authoritative voice, boomed out: 'You lot. Turn it off!' – No 'Please', or 'Do you mind', or 'Would you . . .' but an order; and there was a general murmur of approval.

I kept my head down over my paper – non-involvement, that's me!

'Why should I?' came the reply. I looked up and saw it was the biggest of the three young men speaking; and he was a very big, tough-looking young man. Oh dear, I thought, there's going to be trouble.

'You heard me! Turn it off!'

'Why? We've paid for our tickets, same as you have.'

Stalemate, I thought.

Then came an even louder, snarling voice: 'You lot. Down in the ghetto department. Get that . . . thing off!' He added a couple of insulting expletives which I won't repeat.

The lads quietly muttered among themselves, then turned the music off. The journey continued peacefully and I sighed a sigh of relief – it could have been nasty.

After a while I decided to go and get a coffee from the buffet, but before I could get to my feet the biggest of the three lads stood up and faced the rest of the carriage. 'I'm going to fetch some coffee now; would any of you – er – gentlemen like me to bring you one?' He made a mock bow. There was not a murmur from the gentlemen, nor from the lady (that's me), who wanted a cup of coffee.

I went for mine later, after a decent interval had elapsed. To tell the truth, I felt a bit ashamed. I'd allowed myself to take sides. I had allied myself with the rude and overbearing. By my silence, I had made it clear that the lads didn't count for anything, were not even worth accepting an offer of help from. I'd been prejudiced by their age, their appearance and their taste in music. I'd allowed them to be verbally abused without uttering a word in their defence – because I was afraid, I suppose, of what the others, who were all unknown to me anyway, would have thought.

I decided I would have a quiet word with the lads at King's Cross, thank them for their forbearance, and apologise for the rudeness of their fellow-passengers. I didn't manage it. They got off at Peterborough.

As they began to gather their belongings I looked up, and the big young man caught my eye. I remembered some words from the Gospel account which described what happened after Peter had denied that he knew Jesus: 'Jesus turned and looked at Peter, and Peter went away and wept bitterly.' I didn't weep. I smiled and said, 'Thank you.' The lad grinned back at me: 'Ta-ra, luv,' then he and his mates were away.

For a brief moment the divide had been crossed, there was communication between two fellow-passengers. But why couldn't I have done it earlier? Why hadn't I said something in the lads' defence? Why hadn't I challenged the rudeness of the other passengers? Whose fault would it have been if one of the lads had punched the bossy man on the nose? Who would have got the blame?

But then these things happen, don't they?

For the whole Law is summed up in one commandment: 'Love your neighbour as you love yourself.' But if you act like wild animals, hurting and harming each other, then watch out, or you will completely destroy one another.
Galatians 5.14–15

Forgive me, Lord, for being such a coward. So often I keep quiet when I should speak up, I am content to go with the crowd rather than ally myself with the minority, I settle for looking respectable rather than show love and concern for the despised. Next time, please give me the courage to stand up for what is right – whatever it costs.

Don't play God!

During the visit of the Queen to China, we were all subjected by the media to a crash course in Chinese, or rather in the Chinese way of life. I found it fascinating seeing all those places and people – although I didn't like the sound of some of the food!

The sad thing for me, though, was seeing the result of the 'one child' rule, that has produced what they call 'the little emperors'. Everything is centred on the one child – the indulgence, the extravagance, the hopes and the demands. What a chilling picture! And sadly, it seems as though the problems associated with that rule are going to increase as those children become adults. They are growing up in an unreal situation.

All right, China has a population problem, like many other countries in the world. The sensible thing was to try to discourage large families and encourage smaller ones, by education and by parents' consent. But by making laws with such tough penalties they have now exchanged one set of problems for a mountain of problems, with worse to come.

But that is China, not this country. Because we wouldn't be so short-sighted, would we?

Well then, what about some of our bright ideas on how to solve our own problems, for instance in housing, education, health or immigration? Some of them, when put into practice, have turned out to be disastrous. The tragedy is that human beings have been seen as things, problems, pawns to be moved here and there and anywhere, to make the graphs and statistics neat and tidy. But people are people, with basic human rights; and everybody should be given the dignity and the freedom to be themselves.

We are all citizens of our country, so we owe it our respect and obedience. I know I have got to do my part in the community. I've got my responsibilities, as you have. After all, we reap the benefits, don't we? But it reminds me of what Jesus said when he was asked whether it was right to pay taxes to an occupying power. He didn't give his questioner the chance to duck out of his responsibility as he replied: 'Render to Caesar the things that are Caesar's,' but added, 'and to God the things that are God's.'

When any state, government or individual takes it upon themselves to play God, doing it with an inflated sense of their own importance based on force, then we all stand in danger. Because so often the result is not heaven on earth, but rather a hell for generations to come. It has happened in the past, and the not too distant past – look at Hitler and Idi Amin. And there are far too many 'little emperors' and tinpot gods strutting round our world at the moment.

I say, let God be God. Let his will be obeyed, his love shared. His way is the best way for all of us. After all, it is his world, and it's about time we all realised that.

The Lord is king.
  He is clothed with majesty and strength.
The earth is set firmly in place
  and can not be moved.
Your throne, O Lord, has been from from the beginning,
  and you existed before time began.   Psalm 93.1–2

Forgive us, Father. We so often try to play God. We forget that you are in control, that it is your world, and our lives must be lived according to your laws, not our ideas. Give us a fresh realisation of your greatness, your power and your love; and make us content to be your children. For Christ's sake. Amen.

Here comes the bride – and groom

I've got a bit of a problem about a wedding! It's my hat, you see. I'm not a hat person, and if you saw me, you'd know why; but I still think big occasions demand one. So that's why there is a hat-shaped cloud on my horizon.

Mind you, the problem of my hat is nothing compared to the real problems of any wedding. The family situations that have to be resolved – like who sits next to whom at the reception. Whether the flowers will arrive on time. Is that photographer *really* reliable? And, worse still, what if the cake is soggy inside? Weddings are 'all go' times, nerves-on-edge times, and tempers tend to get a bit frayed as the big day approaches.

But what about the two at the centre of it all, the bride and groom? Has anyone stopped to consider how they are feeling as they wait to take the plunge? Oh yes, they have been talked to, at and about, been organised and rehearsed. But how are they feeling inside? After all, it's their wedding, not Mum's, or Dad's, Auntie Annie's, or the lady-in-the-funny-hat's. Two young people in love, stepping out in the way God intended for those who want to spend the rest of their lives together, in holy wedlock – an old-fashioned term, but I like it.

It's a terrible risk, is marriage. Just look at the divorce statistics. One in three marriages break up – frightening, isn't it? And the world yells, 'Why bother? Life is too uncertain to be tying yourself down permanently.' And yet, marriage has never gone out of fashion. People still want to get married, and a high percentage still prefer to get married in church.

Why get married in church? The cynics would say it is just rent-a-church, for the scenery, the backcloth to the celebrations. But I've found that most people I know opt to get married in church because they want the assurance of God's blessing. After all, marriage is a very serious and solemn business – fun as well, of course! But those promises! They take some keeping – being faithful, loving, caring, supporting . . . I'm sure most couples mean the promises they make, but they do need help to keep them as the years roll by. Lots of couples will be taking the step in the next few days, like Steve and Margaret (theirs is the one I am going to). I'm hoping and praying that all of them will not just start out by asking God's blessing, but will continue to ask for his help and guidance in their marriage every day.

You know the song – 'Love and marriage go together like a horse and carriage'. That's probably true, but I've found as well that, when God is invited to share in the marriage, then the wheels go round a lot smoother. Well, that's my experience – and I've been married for twenty-seven years.

'In the beginning, at the time of creation, "God made them male and female," as the scripture says. "And for this reason a man will leave his father and mother and unite with his wife, and the two will become one." '
                                                              Mark 10.6–8'

Father, thank you for your gift of human love, for lives shared in marriage, for promises made. May each couple find joy and fulfilment in keeping those promises, and grow in love for each other and for you every day of their lives. Amen.

A world away

South Africa is a long way from Selby, the small town where I live, fifteen miles south of York. A long way, not just in terms of miles, but of climate and culture, experience and expectation. I don't see any giraffes or rhinos as I drive along our country lanes. Our local hill, Brayton Barff, is just a pimple compared with the magnificent Drakensberg Mountains. The coastline of Natal is very different from our seaside resorts of Scarborough and Bridlington. We don't even have many black or coloured people here – I suppose the vast majority of the people who live in this area are Yorkshire born and bred for several generations back. The power stations and the new Selby coalfield have brought in new people, but as it happens they are mainly white British. I suppose *we* were sort of foreigners when we came here from across the Pennines, but we were welcomed, made to feel at home and accepted for ourselves, as I'm sure any newcomers would be. I wouldn't want to live anywhere else. Selby is my sort of town, my sort of people – a good place to be.

So it's hard really to imagine what is going on in South Africa. It's all so different out there, we suppose – the people are different, they think differently, act differently. I was talking recently to someone who only a few days ago came back from there. She is a Christian Aid worker, and she had actually been present when the headquarters of the South African Council of Churches were being raided by the police. She saw the files being taken away, including all the Christian Aid records. She was able to give me an eye-witness account of Christian ministers and other people being carted off to jail, of the disruption of church services and social work. Of

31

young people and children being deprived of their schooling.

As she was describing it, I thought of our own Council of Churches in Selby, of my church of St James', the vicar and all our congregation, of the other ministers and Christian folk in the town – because we all know each other; we're just like a family. I tried to imagine what it would be like if what is happening in South Africa happened in Selby. What would I do, given those circumstances? I've got to be honest – with my temperament I'd probably lash out to protect myself, rush to the defence of my friends, and stand up for what I believe to be right. I wouldn't give in without having a go. But then, it wouldn't happen here, it's not that sort of place. Selby is Selby. South Africa is a long way away – or is it?

Those South Africans, black and white, are just as much my brothers and sisters as my friends in Selby. I must be prepared to help them. But how? I don't even know all the facts, and my attitude is influenced by what I read and hear, and by the way I'm made; the way I react is conditioned by my upbringing.

I read a letter the other day from someone living in South Africa, written to friends in Yorkshire. It ended with these words: 'Please pray for all of us. None of us can help the colour of our skin, but we can help our attitudes. Pray God they will be the right ones.'

So there is no difference between Jews and Gentiles, between slaves and free men, between men and women; you are all one in union with Christ Jesus. Galatians 3.28

Lord, I don't know what's going on in South Africa, but I know what they need. I know what I need, as well. It is understanding, forgiveness, peace. Please give these gifts to all your children. Amen.

Why do they do it?

The other evening my husband and I went out for a meal to a pleasant little town, nestling amongst the hills, the sort of place you see on Beautiful Yorkshire calendars. The car park was just off the main street, well laid out, with trees around it, and perhaps twenty or so cars in it.

We returned after a very enjoyable meal to find the car aerial had been twisted and ripped off, and left beside the car. We were not very pleased, to say the least, but as Peter said, 'I suppose we should count ourselves lucky that whoever did it, didn't do any more damage,' and I was very relieved it had been the aerial that went, not a wheel.

Who did it? Why did they do it? Why choose our car? After all, they didn't know us, and our car is a very ordinary one – nothing to attract attention. But as Peter says, we were lucky. And, glancing through the newspaper day by day, I know we are. Every day there are reports of property destroyed, walls defaced, cars immobilised, and every variety of senseless vandalism; and for every one reported there must be dozens like ours, where the owners say nothing and make good the damage.

I used the word senseless, and so it is. There is no point in these things, is there? Is it that the people who commit these crimes are sick, frustrated, depressed, angry? Is it a cry for help, or a way of kicking against society in general and whatever happens to be there at the time in particular? Is it done just for a laugh, or out of sheer boredom?

Vandalism is one of the chronic diseases of our day, whether on the football terraces or in the streets, and it seems mostly to be committed by young, strong males. I find it very sad that energy is being used in such a negative, aggressive way. If only it could be channelled into something good and constructive.

So what can I do about it? Support the splendid schemes – and there are many of them – to encourage creative action? Lend a sympathetic listening ear to the frustrated youngsters who hang around? Lobby the local M P and ask him to try to influence the government to create more jobs? Or join a neighbourhood watch scheme? Any or all of these things could help, and I reckon all of us could do more in our own communities.

But I'm a Christian, and one of the things that Jesus said was, 'Pray for those who persecute you.' Now, whether having your car aerial broken is persecution, I'm not sure. But I do know how I felt towards the person who did it, and two wrongs don't make a right. So, although it might sound naive, and perhaps of little use, I prayed for the aerial snapper, and asked God to show him that he mattered, and that he didn't have to resort to violence to prove it.

All right, maybe I'm soft. Maybe if it had been the wheel I would have felt different. Maybe if I knew all the facts . . . But then, the strange thing is that praying helped me. It helped me realise that, although I don't go round snapping aerials or the like, I equally need understanding and forgiveness and help – like we all do, don't we?

'You have heard that it was said, "Love your friends, hate your enemies." But now I tell you: love your enemies and pray for those who persecute you, so that you may become the sons of your Father in heaven.'   Matthew 5.43–5

Lord, why do they do such stupid things? Why do they cause so much misery by their disregard of people and property? They make

me angry, they are downright sinful, they deserve to be punished.
. . . And I am downright sinful, I deserve to be punished. But
you love me, you understand, you forgive. Help me to love, to
understand and forgive others – for your sake. Amen.

Men and women of
courage

When the BBC screened the series of live programmes, *Hospital Watch*, I have to admit I became a television addict. I hadn't intended watching it, but having seen one programme I was well and truly hooked. I found it such compulsive viewing, not because of all the operations – I had to turn away or shut my eyes when some of those were shown, but because we saw such marvellous people. The dedicated hospital staff, all of them working together, the way they put all they had into caring for people. And the patients – the courage and cheerfulness they showed, the complete lack of resentment and bitterness, even though many of them had to undergo major surgery, and others were having extensive treatment for various conditions. There was no trace of envy of those who were walking around fit and well while they were having to cope with so much. There was one lady suffering from bone cancer. She must have been in a lot of discomfort, yet she was so thankful for life and for her family and friends, and she had a really radiant smile as she spoke of her faith in God.

And isn't it amazing what can be done today, especially through surgery. I watched the kidney transplant operation and saw the donated kidney, frozen and white, transplanted into the man who would probably have died without it – and immediately it became soft and pink and doing its job. As the surgeon said, so wryly, 'One moment that kidney was a piece of useless offal, the next a living organ.' To see that happening, was to witness a miracle – no one can ever tell me that miracles don't happen today!

Seeing that kidney transplant reminded me of someone else who had just such an operation – Police Constable

George Hammond. Remember him? He was the policeman who was stabbed so viciously and nearly died from it. He went through a year of pain and suffering, when it was touch and go whether he would make it; but now with the transplant he is able to lead a nearly normal life again, and get back on duty in the job he loves. But of course, he lost a year of his life, and he could be very bitter about that, especially towards the person who caused it. But do you know what he said? 'I feel no bitterness towards him. If you let bitterness creep into your mind, it becomes soul destroying.'

When I heard that, I felt very ashamed of myself, because I know how many times I get angry and resentful, or I feel bitter when someone lets me down or things don't work out the way I'd hoped for or planned. I get upset over the most trivial and silly things at times, and then make excuses for myself. The result is, I get miserable and bad tempered, tensed up, and am no pleasure to myself or to anyone else.

George Hammond is right, isn't he? Bitterness is soul-destroying. It just makes you twisted and useless. When I get like that, I reckon I'm like that frozen kidney, a bit of useless offal. It is only when I let go of the bitterness and anger, the pettiness in my life, and start being thankful for what I've got, and begin thinking about other people and caring for them, that I warm up and become soft – in the nicest possible way – and can be of some use in the world. And then life is much better for me, too.

Do not pay back evil with evil or cursing with cursing; instead, pay back with a blessing, because a blessing is what God promised to give you when he called you.   1 Peter 3.9

Lord, thank you for all the marvellous people who work in our hospitals, and for the patients who are living examples of courage and hope, faith and forgiveness. Give me grace to show some of those qualities in my life today.

So what is your story?

Having a book published is rather a nerve-racking experience. After all the time spent working on it, burning the midnight oil, then the waiting for it to come out, it is suddenly rather a frightening prospect. What will people think of it? How about the reviews – will they say, 'What a load of rubbish'? Or, worse still, 'What a bore'? But it's the risk writers have to take. I've made myself vulnerable. I am wide open to what anyone says or thinks. I've asked for it.

I remember when I was asked to write my first book, *Called to Be Me*. After the excitement and thrill of being asked to write had worn off, I decided the answer was a definite No. Putting down on paper the story of my life, warts and all – well, I couldn't do it! What on earth would people think of me?

I went to see my bishop at the time; a saintly and wise man. He let me go on at length about why I couldn't write the book, and finally, when I had run out of breath, he said very quietly, 'Margaret, I'd like to ask you just one question. Are you ashamed of what God has done in your life?'

'No,' I said.

'Well, then,' came the firm reply, 'What's your problem?'

Put like that, I realised that I hadn't got a problem. All I had to do was to be honest and open and write it as it was, as I am. It was as I did that, that I realised what God had done for me, the many times he had rescued me from myself, picked me up when I'd fallen flat on my face, prodded me in the right direction, opened doors and pushed me through, given me a caring family, given me friends. Most of all, I realised just how much I mattered as *me*, with all my faults and failings, my stubbornness, my 'I can do it myself' attitude. Yes, he knew all that, and still loved me, and has gone on loving me, and always will.

We are all different. Your story is your story. Maybe you'll never write it down, but it is special, because you are special – unique. You may think you are unimportant, just a cog in the machine, a number. Sadly, society brainwashes us into thinking that. But don't believe it. It's not true. You are some*body*, not some*thing*. Remember that.

There is a verse in the Bible which says this: 'Do not be afraid. I will save you. I have called you by name – you are mine.' These words, from the book of Isaiah, remind us that we do matter, in spite of all that is happening around us, and whatever anyone else says.

What does that mean for you, though? It means that God loves *you*, knows *you*, cares about *you*. He wants you to enjoy life, to get the most out of it and, if you will let him, he will show you how.

As I look back on my life, I'm so glad I didn't try to go it alone, but put my hand into God's hand. Strangely enough, I found as I put out my hand to him, he'd been there all the time, and I just hadn't realised it.

Lord, you call very strange people to follow you, and very ordinary people too; not just the clever, the very religious or those with a good reputation. Your invitation is for anybody, even me! Thank you for calling me to your service. Help me to bring honour to your name.

Bless you!

We were having a few days' holiday in Italy, one of those autumn breaks in the sun. (I can recommend Sorrento, it's a fascinating place, and a delight to explore.) My husband and I were looking at one of the churches on a Sunday morning, and we were just about to go inside when we saw a priest standing by the door chatting to a young and obviously very happy couple. We stood back waiting until they finished their conversation, which we couldn't follow anyway because we don't speak Italian. Then the three of them bowed their heads and the priest prayed. 'I expect they've come to see about getting married,' I said to Peter, 'and he is having a prayer with them. How nice.' Then to our surprise the priest took some holy water out of a container and sprinkled it, not over the young couple, but over the brand new car parked next to them. There were handshakes all round, and the young couple drove away smiling.

I suppose to most of us it seems a bit strange, having a car blessed. But then, why not? Our cars are very much part of our lives, like our homes, our work, and our recreational activities. Churches and public buildings are dedicated; we pray for God's blessing on ships 'and all who sail in them'; and I was recently invited to a ceremony to dedicate a new travelling library van. So why not cars? After all, if you are anything like me, you spend a lot of your time in your car.

But then I got to thinking, as I saw the young couple drive away. Will the fact of their car having been blessed make them more careful drivers? Will they be more courteous, more responsible? Will they take extra care of that vehicle because it is not just a piece of equipment but a sacred trust?

Or will they say, 'We've asked for God's help and protection; now it's all up to him to look after it and us'? Judging by the state of some of the cars we saw in Italy, something has gone sadly adrift!

The same questions apply, I suppose, to those of us who were married in church. We went along and asked for God's blessing. We put ourselves into his care. We made promises, too. And again, those of us who are parents and have had our children baptised – we asked for God's blessing on them, and promised to bring them up in the Christian way.

I suppose it is easy for us to go to one of two extremes. We can think, once the ceremony is over, 'We are on our own now, we've done the religious bit, now we can get on with living our lives, and bringing up our children in our own way.' Or maybe we put all the onus on to God. We've handed over our marriage, our children, or both, we've got the bits of paper to prove it, so now it's up to God to protect us, to keep us out of trouble. If anything goes wrong, God gets the blame, one hundred per cent.

I've got the sort of mind which retains slogans, and one that sticks in my mind is, 'It all depends on me, and I depend on God.' Somehow it puts in a nutshell what life is about for me. It reminds me of my responsibility. I've got to use my brain, and my heart. I've got to exercise self discipline. But there's someone who will help me get it right, give me the grace to admit my need of help, and set me on the right path again.

Yes, 'It all depends on me, and I depend on God.' I can't speak for the Italian couple, or for you; but for me, Margaret Cundiff, car driver, wife, mother and lots of other things, it's a pretty good recipe – any day.

May the Lord bless you and take care of you;
May the Lord be kind and gracious to you;
May the Lord look on you with favour and give you peace.

Numbers 6.24–6

May the Lord bless and guide and use us,
each and every one!

Someone special

It was a wonderful, joyful, never-to-be-forgotten day. I'd looked forward to it for so long, hardly daring to believe it would actually come at all. It was like an extra special birthday, which, when you come to think about it, describes it perfectly – a birthday, a new start, a new me. It was the day when I, with twenty-seven other women, was ordained deacon in the Church of England.

I was thrilled to receive so many cards and letters, many of them from complete strangers, who wrote assuring me of their love and thoughts, and prayers. The children at Wistow school, where I go to take assembly, sent me a big bag of cards, all their own work. There were pictures of bells, churches, angels, books, dogs, and portraits of me. A gorgeous one showed me dropping into York Minister by parachute. Another had a book design with the title, *Teach Yourself to be a Reverend*. One showed me running along saying, 'I've made it at last,' and a message 'You're still young'! But the one which touched me most was from a little boy called Craig, who wrote on his card, 'Well done, Mrs Cundiff. I wish I was as special as you.' I decided I must have words with young Craig, for he needs to know that he *is* special, just as special as anyone else – because he is himself.

Craig is not alone in wistfully looking at other people and thinking, 'I wish I was as special as him or her.' A lot of people feel like that. One week on *Pause for Thought* I said that some people think they are only cogs in a machine, and a lady wrote to me to say that when she was on holiday in Holland she had to buy a new gear box for the car because a cog had broken off and got entangled in the works – a very

43

expensive business. 'Cogs *are* important,' she wrote. 'It's a matter of knowing one's place in the scheme of things.'

She's right, of course. But that phrase 'knowing one's place' smacks of the old days when servants were told that, meaning, '*You* belong at the bottom of the pile, below stairs.' God doesn't have upstairs and downstairs folk, upper or lower classes, first or second class citizens. He has children – precious, loved, valuable, special – like young Craig, and you, and me. We have a dignity, a unique place in the world, and it is a matter of recognising that; not going round grovelling and being ever so 'umble like Dickens' Uriah Heep, who was actually a proper pain in the neck!

We need to accept ourselves, to discover our gifts and use them, enjoy them, share them. We need to make the most of our opportunities, and to be ourselves. Of course, it is a risky business. We can fall flat on our face. We are open to kicks as well as applause, criticism as well as approval. But then, that's what life is all about – being participants, not spectators.

Jesus came to show us that everybody matters; read the Gospel accounts. He was for everybody. He offered friendship and help – and then said, 'Now you've got a job to do, to treat others as I have treated you, as important, as people.' He said, 'This is my command, that you love one another as I have loved you.'

It is only as we realise that we are special to him, that we can see other people as special too – and that means *everybody* – with no exceptions.

'For only a penny you can buy two sparrows, yet not one sparrow falls to the ground without your Father's consent. As for you, even the hairs of your head have all been counted. So do not be afraid; you are worth much more than many sparrows!'   Matthew 10.29–31

Father, to know I matter to you so much, is marvellous. I can hardly believe it, and yet it is true. Will you remind me that other people are just as important as me to you as well, because I forget that fact so easily. Amen.

What future for youth?

One of the questions I was asked most frequently when I was a youngster was, 'What are you going to be when you grow up?' My answers varied from the down-to-earth 'typist' or 'teacher' to flights of fancy when I saw myself as an opera singer or a Member of Parliament. I remember one time most of my friends were planning to be ballet dancers, but I knew, even with the wildest stretch of the imagination, that I could never be one of those! I did once have a bit part in a school play as a fairy, but when I look back on that episode in my life, I realise I was very badly cast.

Whatever our aims and ambitions, though, we never had any doubt that we had a future. There was work to be had, and we knew we had a good chance of getting a job if we tried. Many of my friends followed their parents into a trade that their families had been in for generations, and for youngsters like me who had no real idea, it was fairly easy to try a number of jobs before finally settling to one. I was an apprentice cook, paintress, junior clerk and costing clerk in less than three years!

That question, 'What are you going to be when you grow up?' is not a question to be asked today. Young people have no certainty of getting a job, any sort of a job; and the future looks bleak. So what can they do – the out-of-work teenager, the redundant twenty-year-old? What sort of future can they look forward to? Or is it a full stop, a dead end? Is life worth bothering about at all?

I read recently in the local paper that a growing number of jobless youngsters are dabbling in the occult. A Yorkshire vicar who is an exorcist says, 'The jobless, especially the young, are turning to spiritualism, ouija boards and tarot cards to try to look into the future,' and someone who actually makes money out of this as a consultant confirms this is so. He says, 'People are turning more to paganism and the occult because of the growing demands of society, and disillusionment with the Christian religion' – and he throws out a challenge to the clergy to come up with an answer. Whan an indictment!

I find this situation tragic. Young people have enough problems to cope with today without dabbling in things which can cause them even more distress. But then, whose fault is it if they are driven to such desperate measures? The government? The economists? Parents? Teachers? The Church? Or is it that those who could help, don't, and the ones who could lend a listening ear are deaf to their cries for help?

Something I learned all those years ago as a teenager was that God loved me; I mattered to him. Whatever job I got or didn't get, whether I became a high flyer, an also ran, or even a non-starter, I still mattered as *me*. I admit I have had some tough times and disasters over the years, but the fact of God's love, and being able to turn to him, has made all the difference. He doesn't guarantee jobs, or success, but he does guarantee to stick by you, and knowing that has made all the difference to me. I didn't need a crystal ball or a pack of cards to discover that, because there were folk around who not only told me about God's love and care, but showed it to me in their lives.

'I am the light of the world,' Jesus said. *'Whoever follows me will have the light of life and will never walk in darkness.'*　　　　*John 8.12*

Lord, there are so many people who see no sign of hope, no light in their lives. They are desperate to know if there is any future. Help me to bring the good news of your love to one of them today. Amen.

Enjoy yourself!

A friend and I went to see the film *The Name of the Rose*, the medieval murder mystery set in a monastery. Someone remarked that you needed a strong stomach to watch it, and it was a bit like that – rather gory in parts – but it kept me on the edge of my seat.

An interesting point that came through the film was that most people in medieval times thought that Christianity was meant to be one hundred per cent solemnity, a heavy burden to be borne. Faith was something to be endured rather than in any way to be enjoyed. In fact the monks looked, if you'll pardon the expression, as miserable as sin.

Then along came the Franciscan Brother William, played by Sean Connery, and he challenged this viewpoint. He had a sense of humour all right, and an enjoyment of comedy, and he actually laughed. He was sternly rebuked by the gloomy abbot who said, 'We are told in Scripture that Jesus wept. It does not say that he laughed.' To which Brother William replied with a smile, 'And it doesn't say that he didn't.' That remark did not go down too well!

I find that some people today still have the idea that to be a Christian you have to be deadly serious, rather dull and pompous, and must never be seen to be enjoying yourself. Sadly, sometimes the Church gives that impression. No wonder people get frightened off, when looking miserable seems to be almost a virtue, with a catalogue of 'donts' rather than an invitation to enjoy life.

Maybe it doesn't say in Scripture that Jesus laughed; but reading between the lines, I'm sure he did. He attracted people like a magnet. Crowds would go without food just to hear him. Mothers brought their children to him to be blessed. He was invited to a wedding, to feasts and to suppers. You could say that he was the life and soul of many a party. So much so, that one of the accusations against him was that he was a glutton and a drinker, a friend of tax collectors and outcasts – a bit of sour grapes there on the part of his accusers! I'm sure Jesus was great company. He loved people. He enjoyed making them happy and whole. In fact, that is why he came, as he said, so that people might 'have life, and have it in abundance'; might live rather than exist.

I remember some words on judgement that I read once: 'One day we will all be called before God to give account of our lives, and he will call us to account for failing to enjoy the good things he has given us.' God has given us the world, has given us life, has given us other people. He has given us Jesus. It is our own fault if we don't take advantage of his gifts and enjoy them. For in spite of everything, the world is a wonderful place if we will look and listen. And most people are a pleasure to be with if we take the trouble to get to know them, to understand them. And here's a little tip – a smile works wonders. Try it!

When the Lord brought us back to Jerusalem,
  it was like a dream!
How we laughed, how we sang for joy!
  Then the other nations said about us,
  'The Lord did great things for them.'
Indeed he did great things for us;
  how happy we were!   Psalm 126.1–3

Thank you, Father, for all the joy of life – for laughter, for fun, for friends to share our joys. Thank you for all the great things of life, and the greatest joy of all, for Jesus – thank you.

Built to last

I've known Alison since she was a small girl in Sunday School. I've watched her grow up, through school to work, to meeting and falling in love with Michael and then getting married and building up their home together. A few months ago Michael very shyly explained why Alison wasn't in church with him that evening. 'She's not very well,' he said, and then added, beaming, 'but she's not ill.'

The penny dropped. 'You're going to be a dad,' I said.

Michael's smile went from ear to ear, and I rejoiced over good news.

Then one Saturday morning Michael bounded towards me, absolutely glowing with pride. 'Alison had a little girl last night. She and Laura Claire are both very well.' He was ecstatic about it all, and then, looking very serious, he said, 'It's almost unbelievable, isn't it, that two people can meet, fall in love, get married, and then there's someone else, tiny and perfect, who belongs to them.'

I agree. Love, marriage, a child – that's how it should be; that is God's intended way, a recipe for happiness. Michael's face showed the reality of it and later, when I visited Alison and Laura in hospital, I rejoiced with them.

That same week I watched some television programmes on AIDS. They were all very technical, educational and clinical. They left nothing to the imagination, and no youngster, or not-so-youngster, could say that they hadn't been warned about the dangers, and told about the protection that is available. The publicity has certainly made us all aware of the importance of 'being safe, staying safe'. We have become all too aware of the tragedy of AIDS, the needless deaths of

50

young people, the terrible grief of relatives and friends. Talking to people of all ages and opinions, I think the message has got through; it is not something to be treated lightly.

So maybe many deaths will now be avoided if only people will take precautions – and that is a good thing; but it is terribly sad that the campaign has been necessary, because the virus is so rampant. Sad, because young people are tempted to think that as long as they take precautions, they can go on in the lifestyle which gives them satisfaction. I can't help thinking of Alison and Michael and their joy in each other and in that precious gift of a baby daughter. They have set about their lives in God's way, in the right order: love, marriage and a child – and that child now has the benefit of two loving parents, of a family life based on God's recipe for living.

There is a story Jesus told of two men who built identical houses; the difference was the unseen foundations. One built on sand, the other on rock. When the storm came, the difference was revealed; but then it was too late for the house built on the flimsy foundation – it crashed, and was destroyed.

All right, you may say, with the AIDS warning the crash is averted; you needn't die of AIDS now, you can live how you want, safely. But what is the best way? Michael and Alison have got their foundations right. They will be able to survive the storms, built on the rock of obedience to God and love for each other.

It might be worth examining our own foundations for life, from time to time, to check we have got the genuine article, and not a shifting substance.

Each one must be careful how he builds. For God has already placed Jesus Christ as the one and only foundation, and no other foundation can be laid.　　　　1 Corinthians 3.10–11

Father, thank you for the gift of life, and thank you that in Jesus you have given us a sure foundation to build our lives upon. May we never settle for worldly extravagances rather than lasting values, or the thrills of the moment rather than the joys of eternity. We ask it in the name of Jesus Christ, our Rock. Amen.

Tug of war children

I pass a large advertising hoarding on my way into Selby from home. I don't normally take much notice of it; I've usually other things on my mind, like my shopping list, who I'm going to see, or whether I'll catch my local train. So adverts for coffee or cars, lager or the latest petrol station offers, are given but a fleeting glance and forgotten. I'd not make a very good police witness.

But a few weeks ago I did notice an advert. It said, 'Since you passed this poster yesterday another 436 children got divorced.' Four hundred and thirty-six – that's the size of an average school! It really bothers me, and now every day as I pass that poster I look at it and think of those 436 children added to the list since yesterday. Oh yes, I had known the statistics – that one in three marriages ends in divorce, one in eight children live in one-parent families. But that total of children affected by the split up of their parents really shocked me. It brought home to me just what is happening to family life in our country. 'There's no place like home,' says the old song. But what are many homes like today, where there is bitterness, anger, violence both physical and mental, with the resulting breakdown of relationships? Home ought to be a place of security and love. Sadly, for an increasing number of children, it is anything but.

I ask myself, What sort of hope is there for the future, for children who haven't known what it is like to be part of a happy, secure family, with parents who set an example of love and understanding? What is experienced in childhood can make or mar lives for ever. So what is the answer?

I reckon it is up to all of us to try a bit harder in our own family life; to ensure that our children get a decent start, and are given the love and security they need. After all, they didn't ask to be born. They are our responsibility. And if, sadly, yours is a one-parent family, you have got to make doubly sure that the children know you love them, and that they are safe. And please, don't unload on to them your bitterness and anxiety about your former partner – after all, it is still their Mum or Dad.

Thank God, there are a lot of organisations which will help with the problem. The advertisement I saw was placed by the National Children's Homes, and there are many others, like the Children's Society, the Mothers Union, the Salvation Army – and of course, there is the local church. If you need help, have you thought of getting in touch with them? After all, the church is the family of God, and you are part of God's family. He is your Father. You belong. And that includes one-parent and two-parent families, and people who are single, or widowed, or divorced or separated, you and me – all of us.

All right, the church isn't perfect – no family is, not even God's! But why not give it a chance? Go along and meet the people who worship there; get to know them. And if you don't feel at home in the first one you try, then try another one. The main thing is that you become part of a family. There's room for everybody in God's family. He says so. The least you can do is give him and the rest of his family the opportunity to help. You'll never know unless you try, will you?

Then Jesus took the children in his arms, placed his hands on each of them, and blessed them.   Mark 10.16

Father, give wisdom and love to all those who have the care of children, that they may show them what it means to be part of a family where each one is valued for themselves. May every child grow up secure in the knowledge that they are loved and wanted; grant them your protection in danger, and your support in need, for the sake of Jesus Christ. Amen.

Watch your tongue

A headline in one of our local newspapers read: 'Rat kills cows'. My first thought was, 'A rat couldn't kill a cow' – but it did; and not just one cow, but eighteen. It seems that a rat had nibbled through a wire on a milking machine, and the cows were electrocuted. Sharp little teeth biting away on a wire out of sight, and the damage was done. It was a disaster for the farmer. The story reminded me of how a church near us had its organ wrecked a few years ago, by mice who had got inside it and eaten away the felt. It cost thousands of pounds to put it right. It is amazing how much damage such tiny creatures can do.

It is not uncommon for major disasters to be caused by very small things. A dropped match, and a block of flats was wrecked by a gas explosion. A cigarette end carelessly tossed away, and a terrible forest fire resulted. A tiny crack in the brake hose led to a fatal car crash; a small misprint in the operating instructions caused an entire operation to collapse.

During the last war there was a slogan: 'Careless talk costs lives.' We were warned to be on our guard at all times in case something we said was picked up and used by the enemy. 'Careless talk costs lives' is something we should all still bear in mind. We are all guilty. It is so easy to pass on second-hand information, drop hints which have no foundation in truth, jump to conclusions and repeat them as though they were gospel truth. By insinuation, even our tone of voice or facial expression can convey quite the wrong meaning, which is then passed on, losing nothing in the telling. Like those sharp little teeth of the rat on the wire, the damage is done. Some people have even been driven to suicide through whispering campaigns, gossip, hearsay and careless talk. I wouldn't do it, nor would you, if we stopped to think about the possible consequences. But the trouble is, we don't stop to think; we just go on nibbling away, destroying bit by bit. We speak without thinking, 'without due care and attention', and we wouldn't hurt anyone for the world. But the damage is done.

St James described the tongue as a fire – what a good description! He said, 'Just think how large a forest can be set on fire by a tiny flame. And the tongue is like a fire. No one has ever been able to tame the tongue. We use it to give thanks to our Lord and Father and also to curse our fellow-man, who is created in the likeness of God.' Strong stuff, that. But James is right. Maybe he had suffered from wagging tongues, and been bitten.

We all talk too much; I am as guilty as the next person. I need to watch my words. It is so easy to hurt people without thinking. It is just carelessness, thoughtlessness – but it is lethal. If only we would think before we speak! For our words *could* bring comfort and healing, and give so much pleasure. We could repair damaged lives, or bring people together. We could, and we would, if we only stopped to think.

May my words and my thoughts be acceptable to you,
O Lord, my refuge and my redeemer!   Psalm 19.14

57

Judge not!

When I was invited over to Ireland to take some meetings and preach, I met some marvellous people, both in the North and in the South. Catholics and Protestants, Christians of all denominations, they gave me a real welcome and were most kind to me. It's not all bad news in Ireland. There are lots of people who do get along well together and help each other, regardless of politics or religion.

I was very taken by a notice I saw outside one church. It said: 'Remember, you never get a second chance to make a first impression.' That stuck in my mind – and I did my best to make a good first impression wherever I went!

It's true, we are often judged on first impressions. People decide whether they are going to bother with us or not, whether we are worth getting to know. They make snap decisions, and often stick to them, even if those first impressions are completely wrong. A man I know got quite upset recently because he thought I was cross with him; I hadn't smiled when I met him. It just so happened that I'd got a lot on my mind, and wasn't concentrating on what I was doing. Fortunately he did tell me, and so I was able to put it right. But it could have spoiled our friendship.

We all make snap decisions. We jump to conclusions about people, and pass judgement on others, often quite unjustly. Like the click of a camera shutter, our minds register an image, and it is posted into our memory and there it stays. It is true, as the poster said – we don't get a second chance to make a first impression. But then, shouldn't we give other people the benefit of the doubt, and give them a second chance, and a third, and more?

Jesus said, 'Do not judge others, so that God will not judge you. For God will judge you in the same way as you judge others, and he will apply to you the same rules you apply to others.' I wouldn't like God to jump to conclusions about me. I'd want to say, 'Give me another chance. It was because I wasn't feeling so well'; or, 'I was miles away'; or, 'I was late for an appointment'; or . . . The great thing is, God does give us a second chance. He goes on giving us chances. And what is more, he understands why we are as we are, even at our most disagreeable. He doesn't judge. He steps in, listens to our moans, and offers us his help. He doesn't write us off, but comes alongside to help us sort out our problems, and puts the smile back on our face, so that we are able to cope with the world – and with ourselves.

So don't be too hasty. Don't jump to conclusions; give the other person another chance. First impressions can be so wrong. Well – take a look in the mirror first thing in the morning. Would you give someone with a face like that a second chance? But God does. So why can't you?

'. . . I do not judge as man judges. Man looks at the outward appearance, but I look at the heart.'   1 Samuel 16.7

Lord, I jump to conclusions, and I pass judgement on others, without knowing the facts, without understanding, and without love. Forgive me, and give me the grace to accept rather than condemn, to encourage not ignore, and always to remember your mercy and compassion which I enjoy and should share with others. Amen.

The loving touch

I read an item in a newspaper recently which disturbed me a lot. It was about a new doll which has been produced by one of the major toy companies. It is a very super doll, so lifelike it could almost be mistaken for a real child. It not only looks right, but feels right; the perfect gift for any little girl. The reason for producing it, say the manufacturers, is that children are looking to their toys more for affection and companionship, in this era of busy working mums and more and more single parent families. The doll has been brought out to ease loneliness.

What I find so disturbing is that I'm sure the manufacturers are absolutely right in their assessment of today's society. Many children are having to look for substitute affection, because they are not being given enough real love and attention. Isn't that sad? Of course, I am not saying there is anything wrong with toys – they are an essential part of life. I've still got my old teddy carefully stored away, and I wouldn't part with him, in spite of his moth-eaten, threadbare frame; and I know plenty of adults, some quite elderly, who have toys. But they are toys, and not people. They are not to be seen as a substitute for human love. If they are, something has gone sadly wrong. I enjoyed my teddy, and my dolls and other toys; but real love came from my parents, friends and family.

It is not only the children today who are seeking substitute love and affection. For many folk, 'things' have replaced people; material goods have taken the place of companionship; and the television or radio, left on all day 'for company', replaces conversation. I came across another newspaper article which was about the need we all have for human contact. It said that lots of people suffer from all sorts of hang-ups and frustrations simply because nobody ever reaches out and touches them, gives them a hug and a kiss. It went on to say, 'In this harsh and cruel world we need a gentle, loving touch more than anything, and a loving touch is a life-enhancing gift both for the giver and the receiver.'

The great gift which Mother Teresa and her nuns bring to the suffering people of Calcutta is that gift of the loving touch; the love and concern which they show for people whom everybody else has written off as of no value. She shows the way of Jesus by practical love and care. Jesus went around caring for individuals. He talked to them, listened to them, blessed and healed them; holding out his arms, touching them with his hands. His touch brought new life, healing and peace.

All right, you may say, but Jesus lived a long time ago, and Mother Teresa is in India. I need someone *now*. But stop and ask yourself, how long is it since you reached out to someone else, or held your hand out in welcome? Or do you keep yourself to yourself and then wonder why you are lonely? If you would take that first step towards someone else, you could find it was a real blessing, not only to another lonely person but to yourself as well.

And what about Jesus? Where is he? The writer of the well-loved evening hymn knew:

Thy touch has still its ancient power,
No word from thee can fruitless fall.
Hear, in this solemn evening hour
And in thy mercy, heal us all.

61

Lord, thank you for your hand upon my life, which makes all the difference to every day. Give me the courage, the love, the will to reach out a helping hand to someone else today, in your name, and for your sake. Amen.

Keep going

The running 'bug' seems to have bitten a lot of people recently. Years ago, it was only the athletic types who ran, those who were intent on getting medals and who wore club vests. Now, nearly everybody seems to go out running.

Well, I don't. I sometimes run for a bus or a train, but nothing so spectacular as getting kitted out and racing round the streets. Mind you, if you saw me, you'd realise why! I wasn't built for running – more a steady idle!

I think what has created and sustained this interest in running for the ordinary person, is the magic of the London Marathon. I always enjoy watching it on television. Of course there are the very serious runners, the professionals, who are looking for the big prize money, or the prestige of winning a medal, or even perhaps of being picked for the Olympics. But it is the also-rans I like to see – those who are running to raise money for charity, who dress up and give us all so much fun. And the greatest of the lot, the 'wheel chair runners'. What an inspiration they are!

Of course, only comparatively few can run in the London Marathon, or the big events; but all over the country there are fun runs. Our town of Selby has them, and so do the local villages, giving anyone the chance to compete, to raise money for the local church, or Scout troop, or hospital, or simply to raise a laugh – which is no bad thing in itself. Most of the runners are not aiming to come in first – they know their limitations – but they do aim to complete the course; and you can see by their faces what it means to them to get over the finishing line, even if they are last and everyone else has got changed and gone home for dinner by the time they have made it! Stickability is what counts – completing the course they had set out on.

Stickability – if only there were more folk who had it. How many people start things, make promises, and then give up. It happens in the church as well as anywhere else, and it is so disappointing. Promises, promises – but no results. St Paul, at the end of a long and very difficult life, was able to write to his young friend Timothy: 'I have done my best in the race. I have run the full distance, and I have kept the faith.' He was not referring to the local fun run or the Marathon, but to his life of faith – keeping the promises he made to God, living by faith, pressing on even when the going was tough, lonely and painful.

How many promises have you made to God to keep faith – maybe when you were baptised or confirmed, received into membership of a church; or when you cried out to God, 'Please help me, save me, and I'll serve you'? What about those promises now? Or have you dropped out of the race because it has got too tough? Come on, now, get back into training! Start saying your prayers again, reading the Bible, attending worship. Get into the race, and keep going. Fix your eyes on the finishing line.

For it is stickability, not speed, that counts – in the really important things of life.

As for us, we have this large crowd of witnesses round us. So then, let us rid ourselves of everything that gets in the way, and of the sin which holds on to us so tightly, and let us run with determination the race that lies before us. Let us keep our eyes fixed on Jesus, on whom our faith depends from beginning to end. He did not give up because of the cross! On the contrary, because of the joy that was waiting for him, he thought nothing of the disgrace of dying on the cross, and he is now seated at the right-hand side of God's throne.
Hebrews 12.1–2

64

Lord, I started out in the race so well; it didn't seem far, and I was so sure I would do well. Now I'm tired, it seems all uphill, and I keep falling over. Yet I know I should keep going. Please help me. Give me the strength, the ability, the perseverance I need. Remind me that I am not on my own, but part of your team; and with your help I'll make it, and receive your 'well done'. Amen.

Taken for granted

My daughter Alison and I went on a mini-break holiday together to Belgium. It was a 'girls only' holiday, leaving my husband and son to fend for themselves for a couple of days. We had great fun window-shopping, with no one to say, 'Oh, come on, you've seen all those things before,' and although we didn't actually buy much, we certainly enjoyed exploring the shops in Bruges. We kept finding fascinating things we don't get in Britain; even the way they wrap up the chocolates turns them into works of art. It made ours look terribly dull.

But it was interesting, coming back on the boat, to meet lots of people who were coming to England to do just what we had been doing in their country – shopping. They found our shops exciting. They were quite envious of us living here. It reminded me of when we went to Switzerland one year, and we met an Englishwoman who lived there and she said how she missed things like Oxo cubes and custard powder and Bisto. Or the farmer's wife in Denmark who, describing a visit she had made to England, went into ecstasies about our lovely soft bread which was sliced and wrapped. It just goes to show that one woman's dull shopping list is another's Aladdin's cave.

I suppose the most ordinary everyday things do seem a bit dull to most of us. It's because they are always there, part of life. We don't even notice them – until, of course, we haven't got them, or someone discovers them for the first time, and then we begin to look at that dull, everyday product with new eyes.

I reckon it is the same with people. The people who are always around, we take for granted – friends and family, the postman, the man who services our car, the girl who cuts our hair, the shop assistant. These people are always there, just part of the scene. Perhaps it is time we took a fresh look at them, recognised their worth, and said Thank you.

Then, of course, there is God. Most of us take him for granted. We accept that he exists, but we don't give him a lot of thought. He is there to be used in an emergency, but otherwise . . .

It may sound a bit strange, but meeting people who were thrilled and excited to discover things I had thought very dull and commonplace made me think about the way I take God for granted. So I've been giving him a bit more attention lately, and it has made me appreciate just what he has given me, and what he offers me. I wouldn't like to live in a world without Oxo cubes, custard powder, Bisto and sliced bread, but I could manage without them. But I could never manage without God, so maybe saying Thank you to him now and again won't go amiss.

'Give thanks to the Lord, because he is good;
  his love is eternal!'
Repeat these words in praise to the Lord,
  all you whom he has saved . . .
May those who are wise think about these things;
  may they acknowledge the Lord's constant love.

Psalm 107.1–2, 43

Thank you, Lord, for your constant love, the love which has surrounded me all my life. Thank you for the way in which you provide for me every day. Thank you that your love is forever. Help me to show you my thanks, not only with my lips but in my life, by serving you with praise and joy. Amen.

67

Variety is the spice of life

It is said that you can judge people by the newspaper they read. If you read *The Times* you are in the top bracket, and if it is the *Sun*, then you are one of the common herd. But I know people who read both, so I don't know what that makes them. Perhaps they are still looking for their right place in society – or maybe they have found it, and don't care what anybody else thinks, and good luck to them.

I reckon you can tell far more about a person by the magazines they take. I find it fascinating, on trains and buses, watching people absorbed in their magazines; and sometimes it is most surprising what they are reading. That immaculate business man is absorbed in *Motor Cycle News*, the scruffy teenager is avidly reading her *Vogue* – and why has that old gentleman in the corner got his magazine tucked inside his newspaper so I can't see what it is – I have my suspicions!

We have a wide range of magazines in our house – *The Grocer*, *Woman's Own*, the *Church Times*, *My Guy* and *Coarse Fisherman*, plus a few others. As they come through the letter box there is a mad rush for them, with expressions of delight from the interested party, and groans from the others. Each magazine has its own style, format and jargon, to appeal to those who, as my son puts it, are 'into that sort of thing'. They are definitely for the enthusiast.

But having different interests in our family doesn't mean we don't get on with each other. We get on very well. We enjoy doing lots of things together, even though we have our special personal enthusiasms. We are a family, we love each other, we belong together, and our very differences make life far more interesting and rewarding for all of us, even though we tease each other. How dull it would be if we were carbon copies of each other – it's much more fun being different!

And God has made us all different. We are each unique. Do you realise, there is no one in the world just like you – now there's a thought! God has made us different, so he knows our individual strengths and weaknesses, our varying abilities and interests and temperaments. He doesn't label us, or classify us under social group headings. He just goes on loving us as us, because we are part of his family.

God accepts us as we are. And if he does that, then surely we should accept each other, and be interested in each other. We should listen to other people, even when they are going on about their hobby which doesn't turn us on at all. We should be around to give them a helping hand when they need it, and cheer them up when they are feeling down.

And if you are feeling the odd one out, if it seems that no one cares two hoots about you – remember, God knows you, he loves you, he is interested in you. You are special to him. So why not have a chat to him and tell him how you feel? He will be glad to listen, because, you see, you are one of the family.

Lord, you have examined me and you know me.
You know everything I do;
  from far away you understand all my thoughts.
You see me, whether I am working or resting;
  you know all my actions.
Even before I speak,
  you already know what I will say.
You are all round me on every side;
  you protect me with your power.   Psalm 139.1–5

Lord, sometimes I feel no one knows or cares about me, I don't matter at all; no one understands me, or my problems, no one bothers to ask me how I feel. I might as well not exist. You know, though. You are right beside me now. You are listening. You want me to tell you how I feel. You want to help me because you love me as I am. Thank you. Thank you for being my friend, my Saviour and my Lord. Amen.

Why worry?

Did you know there is an organisation known as the Pennsylvania Worry Group? Well, there is. I read about it the other day, and it seems it is a group formed by a professor of psychology in America to study the subject of worry, and find out ways of helping people who worry. It has come up with some very interesting statistics. For instance: 15 per cent of the population spend more than half their waking hours worrying; more than 13 million Americans of eighteen years of age and over suffer from anxiety disorders. And women worry more than men.

The biggest worries in America are over the environment and nuclear war, and people are worrying more today than ever before. Many people who were interviewed admitted spending most of their waking hours, and even some time asleep, worrying.

I wonder whether you are a member of the worry brigade, or in the non-worriers' ranks – the definition of a non-worrier, by the way, is someone who worries less than ninety minutes a day. So it seems that all of us are worried for some, most or all of the time. I remember seeing a poster a while back which said, 'Don't worry, it may never happen', and across it someone had scrawled, 'It already has. What do I do now?'

We all worry about many things – our health, the family, our work, money, big things, little things, a whole host of things, from the state of the world to idiotic personal things – idiotic to other people, but to us very real and very frightening.

Sometimes we worry ourselves sick; at other times we try to hide our heads in the sand and pretend it isn't happening. Ninety-nine times out of a hundred we find out that our worries and fears were quite groundless and we can laugh at ourselves for getting so uptight. But there are times when our worries materialise. What we worried might happen, does. There is a family row; we can't cope with the kids; the girl-friend finds another man; someone we love dies; we don't get the job we hoped for.

That's when we need a friend, a real friend, to help us to cope. Not a genie with a magic lamp who will make our troubles evaporate – life's not like that – but someone to listen, to get alongside us; someone who does understand how we feel.

I find friends a terrific help to me. When I have had problems, when worries have become hard realities, friends have helped to get me through. But the best friend, I've found, is Jesus Christ. He knows about life. He has been through it, and taken all the knocks, and survived. So I just talk to him about it all.

St Peter gave this advice, when writing to some friends of his: 'Cast all your cares on him, for he cares for you.' Now that might seem so simple, too good to be true, almost, that you might think it wouldn't do anything for you at all. But all I say is, Try it. I've found it works, and it has taken me out of the worrying brigade into the non-worriers battalion. Oh, yes, I still worry at times. I still find, sadly, that some of my worries are very real. But I find that Jesus is even more real, and he makes all the difference.

'Do not be worried and upset,' Jesus told them. 'Believe in God and believe also in me.'   John 14.1

Lord, I do worry about all sorts of things. I get so worked up, and then I can't sleep, then I wake up tired, and start worrying again. It becomes a vicious circle of worry. Please help me to trust you for each day, each hour, each moment; to place my worries into your hands, leave them there, and then get on with living. Amen.

Never too late

I had a letter the other day from someone I hadn't seen for over thirty years. We were students together. She was a bit older than I was, and used to try to organise me – always reminding me about the work I should be doing, giving me pep talks, and generally trying to keep me on the straight and narrow. She was a serious, studious type, whereas I – well, I tended to treat life as a bit of a joke. I had a fairly easy-going, or even idle, approach to what I should have been doing, being much more interested in what happened to catch my attention at the moment than in preparing for life ahead. So we did tend to get at cross purposes now and again; but I had forgotten all about that until her letter came.

In the letter she said she had been thinking about me quite a lot, and remembering how she used to push me around and get so impatient with me. She went on, 'Looking back, I realise I wasn't always very kind to you. I know it's a long time ago, but if I did hurt you by my attitude, I'd like you to know I'm sorry.'

Obviously, this had been on her mind for some time, so I wrote back immediately and assured her I hadn't remembered her in that way at all. In fact, I had remembered how good she had been to me, and how she had got me out of some difficult patches; and I had appreciated the way she had mothered me all those years ago. I was sorry she had been worried about it, but I was glad she wrote, because writing and saying 'I'm sorry' had released her feelings of guilt. She had made things right, and she could look back on those days without any pangs of conscience.

We are all guilty of doing and saying things that may hurt

other people. Often we just don't think before we speak; or we've got ourselves a bit worked up about something, and the first person who comes along cops it for all! Then afterwards we are sorry, but we don't actually get round to saying it, and sometimes it bugs us for years: 'If only I hadn't said that.'

It is likely that whoever we upset, or thought we upset, at the time, has forgotten it years ago, or didn't take any notice at the time anyway. But if there is something that is nagging away at you, someone you feel you should apologise to, then drop them a line, or give them a ring. Because it's never too late to say Sorry, never too late to repair a friendship, never too late to let someone know they matter.

Never too late – well, the trouble is, if we keep putting it off, it could be too late. We might not be able to trace the person, or worse still, we might have let the regrets harden into bitterness and depression, to blight our relationships today because of yesterday's mistake. I've found that, if something is troubling me, it is best to deal with it while I have the chance and the inclination – for my own peace of mind as well as anything else. And peace of mind is more precious than hollow pride any day!

Get rid of all bitterness, passion, and anger. No more shouting or insults, no more hateful feelings of any sort. Instead, be kind and tender-hearted to one another, and forgive one another, as God has forgiven you through Christ.   Ephesians 4.31–2

Lord, I've said and done such silly things. I've hurt other people, my friends, and now I am sorry, but it is so hard to apologise. Even now I feel embarrassed, but it was so long ago. Yet I know I should do something. Give me the strength and the grace to apologise, to make a new start with my friends and with you. Amen.

Plastic money can kill

At first I used to think they knew something about me that I didn't. Maybe someone had left me a fortune in their will and I would come into it next year. Or maybe I looked like the sort of person who might be coming into money – some time. *They*, being all those organisations who keep trying to press money and goods upon me. I'm always getting letters telling me I don't have to wait one day longer to have a new car, an extension on the house, an exotic holiday, or cash in my hand so I can go on a mad spending spree. I could get a little plastic card, or even a collection of little plastic cards, pop them in a machine, push the button and, hey presto, I've hit the jackpot!

But then, it's not just me, it's everybody; the offer of 'live now, pay later' is big business, on offer to all. And it really is tempting – and frightening.

It seems that most of us fall for the offers, and in a big way. Eighty-six per cent of us buy goods on credit, and most of us have more than one account. 'Plastic money', it's called. But the trouble is, it has to be repaid in hard cash, and you can't get that out of a machine without paying a great deal for it. It can cost far more than cash, too. Every day there are more and more reports of people getting themselves into a real mess, driven to depression, out of their homes, even into the divorce courts; and sometimes, sadly, even to committing suicide. Oh yes, I admit, not everyone will finish up like that. Most people don't; they are sensible about credit, and keep it within well defined limits. But it is a temptation, when money is short and there is so much we would like, to go for gold – the gold of the credit card.

When we first got married, my husband and I were very hard up; we had the minimum of belongings, and every penny counted. But we had a lot of fun planning what we would have when we'd saved up. I still remember those happy times just looking in shop windows and planning and laughing. It gave us so much pleasure – and what a sense of achievement when we had got enough cash and could pay for something we had set our hearts on! I reckon it did our marriage and our relationship the world of good. We struggled together, we planned together, we waited together – and we got there, in the end.

One of the most precious gifts in life is a sense of freedom – not having burdens round your neck. And, believe me, borrowing money, living on credit, is a burden and a worry. It can spoil life, sour relationships, and even endanger your health. We can all get so tied up with material things, worrying about what we haven't got, or have got, that we forget that the most important things in life are not those you pay cash for. The really important things are qualities like love, and faith, and trust, and beauty, and friendship, and hope . . . as Jesus reminded his friends: 'Isn't life worth more than food? And isn't the body worth more than clothes? Your Father in heaven knows that you need all these things. Be concerned above everything else with the Kingdom of God and with what he requires of you . . .'

It's good advice. I've found it works. Enjoy God's world. Enjoy his love. Look around; there is so much to enjoy. Don't get yourself burdened with debt for things you could have waited for, or done without altogether. Real treasure is without price. You have to work at it, but in the end it lasts for ever.

I know what it is to be in need and what it is to have more than enough. I have learnt this secret, so that anywhere, at any time, I

am content, whether I am full or hungry, whether I have too much or too little. I have the strength to face all conditions by the power that Christ gives me.

Philippians 4. 12–13

Lord, teach me to be content with what I have, rather than striving after what I have not. Show me where true value is to be found, in enjoying the good things you have given me: friendship, the world around, health and strength to enjoy life. Please give me what I need and not what I think I want. And above all, give me a thankful heart. Amen.

Turn it to good account

I had worked out my plan of campaign, and it would suit me fine! I had to go to Cambridge to give a lecture, and as it was many years since I had been there last, I decided to take an earlier train, and spend a couple of hours exploring the city before going on to give the lecture. A good way to mix business and pleasure, I thought.

British Rail decided otherwise. The train from York arrived in Peterborough half an hour late, and I found my connection to Cambridge had gone. I had another hour and a half to wait for the next. There were several of us wanting the connection, so we had a good moan, all to no avail, and then sat down on the platform to wait. Then I thought to myself, 'Why not have a look round Peterborough? It's only over the bridge.' So I deposited my case in the left luggage office and went off on my journey of discovery.

What a beautiful city Peterborough is! It has a lovely cathedral, pretty squares filled with flowers, graceful buildings and a marvellous shopping centre. It was all very pleasant indeed. I really enjoyed discovering a place I'd only ever gone through on the train before.

I returned to the station to find my fellow passengers still sitting glumly on the platform, still complaining and looking bored to tears. I got some strange looks when I enthused about the attractions of Peterborough. They, poor souls, had sat it out, and not enjoyed their view from the platform at all. Trains can get boring, particularly if they are dashing past, and not going your way!

Thinking about it later, I suddenly remembered some words from the Psalms: 'As they pass through the valley of

78

Baca, they make it a place of springs.' Baca – the waterless place, elsewhere described as 'the vale of misery', which became a place of fresh clean water. The Psalmist wasn't talking about British Rail – it was more camels and horses in his day – but the principle was just the same then as now. As we go through life we can either be negative or positive. If we will have the right attitude, trusting God to guide us and show us the best way, then even the disappointments of life can be turned into joy.

Maybe you are going through a dry patch in your life, and it's all rather pointless. Search for the springs; they are there if you will look for them! For me, Peterborough wasn't Cambridge. I had to alter my plan; but if I hadn't been stranded in Peterborough I would never have discovered its beauty and charm. Life's alternatives can sometimes be very rewarding, if we will accept them with grace.

Blessed are the men whose strength is in thee,
  in whose heart are the highways to Zion.
As they go through the valley of Baca
  they make it a place of springs;
  the early rain also covers it with pools.   Psalm 84.5–6

Lord, when I think everything is so dry and dull, remind me about the wells of your love. Show me those springs of freshness and life which are there if only I will look. Thank you for providing springs in my desert; for the living water, there for me to draw on. Amen.

It shows up in the end

I have always been a fan of Mohammed Ali – Cassius Clay as he was when he first began his boxing career. 'I float like a butterfly, sting like a bee,' he proudly boasted, claiming 'I am the greatest.'

Perhaps it surprises you that I should admire such a man in such a profession, but there it is! He was more like a ballet dancer than a boxer as he gracefully danced around his often lumbering opponents. Heavyweight champion of the world three times over, he was, as he said, 'the greatest'. I liked him. I admired the way he had risen from nothing to be a world figure. I admired his persistence, the way he proved his critics wrong; and I must admit, I admired his cheek! The underdog who became a champion, the stuff dreams are made of – a charismatic figure indeed.

Now he is suffering from Parkinson's syndrome, brought on, say his doctors, by the injuries he suffered during his twenty-two years in the ring. The damage never showed on him during his fighting career, unlike some boxers who sport cauliflower ears, broken noses and scarred faces. No, he remained unmarked, untouched, so it seemed. Yet the damage was done. It was occurring inside, and now he is a very sick man. I hope he will be able to live with dignity and grace for the rest of his life, for whatever you may think about boxing, he is a great character.

His lifestyle has caught up with him, taken its toll. And what is true for him is surely true for us all. How we live affects our health – body, mind and spirit. Our attitudes, the way we think, our relationships, are all factors in what sort of person we are and become. Bitterness, tension, anger, guilt, fear, envy – all these things can warp our personality. They can destroy us if we are not careful. Broken noses and cauliflower ears are nothing compared to broken hearts and closed ears. What we are matters far more than what we look like, for in the end it is the real you and I who will stand before God – and not the cosmetic concoction we try to kid ourselves we are.

Fill your minds with those things that are good and that deserve praise: things that are true, noble, right, pure, lovely and honourable.

Philippians 4.8

Lord, I go to so much trouble about the way I look. I want to look good, to be admired, so I cultivate my image, with the aid of the beauty counter. Yet you see what I am really like inside. You know the ingredients that make up my inner self. Please cleanse, heal and renew my spirit, that I may be beautiful for you. Amen.

Sunday is special

It's Sunday again. How the weeks roll by! Sunday is the day that separates the weeks, and in spite of all the changes over the years, Sunday is still a different day from all the others.

When I was a child, Sunday was very quiet. There were no buses and no shops open, apart from the corner paper shop which opened for an hour or so in the morning. I used to fetch my dad's newspaper from there before I went off to Sunday school and church.

I looked on Sunday as a mixed blessing. The best things were the meals, especially dinner. We were pretty hard up, but Mum always made sure there was a roast on Sunday, with plenty of home-grown vegetables and fruit. And Sunday tea wouldn't have been complete without a special cake. Sometimes we had tinned fruit as well, with evaporated milk – the smell of evaporated milk still reminds me of those Sunday teas back in Cheshire.

On Sunday afternoons we always went for a walk – down to the town, round the park and back by the canal. I was given a bag of sweets, which I always made last the whole of the afternoon. What I didn't enjoy was having to wear my best clothes and look tidy. I would have much preferred my comfortable, everyday clothes. And the other thing was that I wasn't allowed to walk on the walls, or pick flowers, on Sunday. I never found out why; I was just told I couldn't, because it was Sunday.

Then of course there was Sunday school and church. I went through stages of liking or disliking going but, however I felt, I had to go. I was sent. I have a suspicion that it was to get me out of the way while Mum got the dinner and Dad

82

read his *News of the World* – which was put away from my childish eyes when I came home, although I'd read most of it when bringing it home from the shop!

Yes, it was an old-fashioned Sunday, a long-gone Sunday, not like they are today with all the noise, the traffic, blaring radios, shift work. In fact, Sunday has become almost like any other day. Almost, but not quite. It still has an air about it. It still divides the week up. And there is still church, and people who go to church. Now, I go to church because I want to; because I like to. I look forward to going.

I was taking school assembly the other day with some five-to eleven-year-olds. They were very curious about the kind of work I did. They soon decided that I only worked on Sundays, so I asked them what they thought I did for the rest of the week. There was a silence, then a small boy piped up, 'Practise your words.'

Well, I reckon there was an element of truth in that, because I do prepare for Sunday all week – but I do a lot more besides! I usually take two services each Sunday, and preach at them, so there is quite a lot of preparation to do. Sometimes it is a very informal sort of service, a family service, often with a baptism – and usually I find the baby who is being baptised is the best behaved in church. I don't mind the noise, though; family services are great fun. We do family things, like singing Happy Birthday to You for anyone who has had a birthday that week. We have quizzes, and we let the children and young people take the prayers, read the lessons and lead the singing. Sometimes we have a bit of drama, or a special music item; or someone will share with us what is going on in their organisation, or give a book review; or we have a missionary spot. We always finish up by having coffee and biscuits (orange juice for the children) served in the pews. In the summer we often go out for a picnic lunch together or spend the afternoon in the park. It is a real family occasion, and great fun.

If I have a favourite service, though, it is the Holy

Communion – Eucharist, Mass, the Lord's Supper, different churches call it by different names – but what it is, is being reminded by the visual aids of bread and wine just how much God loves us; that Jesus died for us, and shed his blood for each one of us. Actually seeing and receiving the bread and wine makes it so much more real to me; it brings it all home in a special way. As I share the bread and wine with my church family, it reminds me what it means to be part of the family of God. It doesn't matter who we are or what we are; we are all equal, we are all welcome, we all belong. We are invited to share in it by Jesus himself. I find that quite mind-blowing – being invited to share in the meal with him, and with all his other friends.

So, you see, I enjoy Sunday, every Sunday. I look forward to sharing with others in praising God, in worship, in music and silence, in fun and in meditation; with bread and wine. And yes, with coffee and biscuits and even with soggy sandwiches in the park. For me, it is a foretaste of heaven. For one day, every day will be Sunday. Now there's a thought!

'Observe the Sabbath, and keep it holy. You have six days in which to do your work, but the seventh day is a day of rest, dedicated to me.'
Exodus 20.8–10

Thank you, Lord, for the day that is different. Thank you for Sunday. Thank you that it still calls us to stop and think about our lives, about where we are going and what we are doing. Thank you that it reminds us of you. Help us, every Sunday, to take our eyes and minds off ourselves for a while, and listen to you.

Hands up!

One of my favourite hymns is 'Guide me, O thou great Jehovah', preferably sung by the Treorchy Male Voice Choir. There is power in those voices – big, strong men singing their hearts out in praise of God. I find it very moving and exciting.

I like hymns, particularly the rousing sort. I suppose most people do – that is why programmes like Sunday Half Hour and Songs of Praise are so popular, even with people who don't go to church or who wouldn't call themselves religious.

Some time ago I was at a church service attended mainly by people who could neither speak nor hear; they were deaf and dumb. The singing was marvellous; everybody joined in. It was led by a deaf choir, with a few of their friends, and they all signed the hymns with their hands. It was a tremendous experience. I was in no doubt what the words were and what they meant, and the hymns came over to me in a new and dramatic way. I saw them as well as heard them, and that made all the difference.

We all express ourselves with our hands. I know I do, when I'm preaching and even when I am talking on radio. I can't help it. We hold out our hands in friendship; we protect ourselves with our hands; we push people away or hold them close; we hit out in anger or soothe someone who needs help. We can use our hands for good or ill, as signs of love and affection or of hatred and anger.

We can tell a great deal about people by their hands – the sort of work they do, the lives they lead. A pianist's hands may look a great deal different from a gardener's, yet both equally are used to create something beautiful. A new baby's hands are small and delicate and perfect; an old person's worn hands tell a story of work and of age, marked by experience.

Have a look at your own hands. What do they reveal about you? God gave you those hands. How are you using his gift? Are you the first to respond when someone says, 'Give us a hand, will you?'; or are they pushed down inside your pockets? Are they the sort of hands which reach out to help? – or to grab what you think is yours, or ought to be?

Think about the hands that have helped you in your life. The hands that brought you into the world. The hands that helped you grow up; the hands that make life easier for you now. We all rely on other people's hands far more than we realise. The trouble is, we all take hands for granted – our own and other people's.

When my mother was a girl, times were very hard – much harder than they are today, even – and she thought herself fortunate to get a job as a kitchen maid when she left school. She was what was known as a skivvy. It was not much of a life, working long hours in harsh conditions, for little pay. She told me how her hands became chapped and covered in chilblains through scrubbing – red, raw and bleeding, and very painful. She said that when she went home, her mother took her hands and cried over them, because she wanted her daughter to have a better life, but couldn't give it to her. Yet, my mother says, 'I didn't mind the scrubbing because I knew the bit I earned would help out at home, and so it was worth it.' She loved her mum and would have done anything for her, and her hands said it all. Her hands said, 'I love you,' and her mother's tears on those hands said the same, 'I love you.'

When Jesus was on earth he used his hands to help others. His were strong, workman's hands, for he was a carpenter by trade. They were gentle, loving hands, too, reaching out to help, to heal, to comfort, to encourage. He laid his hands on people who desperately needed help – the leper, the outcast, the sick and the anxious. He picked up children, cradled them in his arms, and blessed them. He held out his hands in friendship to those whom no one else wanted to know, the people others turned away from, or looked down on. In the end, those hands of his were nailed to a cross, and he was hoisted up to die a slow, lingering, painful death. Not much of a reward for loving service, was it? Yet even on the cross he stretched out the hand of friendship to the criminal beside him: the hand of forgiveness to those who had nailed him there; and the hand of love to his mother and his friends stood by the cross weeping, broken-hearted and helpless.

Why did he do it? What good did it do? At the school where I go every week to take assembly, we often sing, 'He's got the whole world in his hands'. It has a cheerful tune that makes me want to have a little dance. But I was brought down to earth one morning after we had sung it, when a small boy asked, 'Mrs Cundiff, if God has got the whole world in his hands, why do nasty things happen?'

I tried my best to explain that often *people* are responsible for the nasty things that happen, and that just being in the world means that we are subject to the bad things as well as the good things that happen, and it is not God's fault. But the little lad was not convinced – because, of course, he had asked the question everybody asks as they look at the world, and it doesn't seem to have an answer. You may find it hard to be convinced that God's hand is on the world as you see all the evil and sin, the people who are suffering through no fault of their own, those who just haven't a chance, or those who have been struck down by illness and disease – and maybe as you look at your own problems and difficulties.

All I can say is, that I know God has got us all in his hands because of what Jesus did on the cross. Those outstretched hands say, 'I love you.' I know, too, that death was not, and is not, the end, because Jesus rose from the dead. He came to his friends when he had risen from the dead, and showed them his hands, and blessed them, and assured them, and all who will trust him, that new life has been secured by his hands. His love, his life, are the proof. We are safe in his hands, for ever.

No, I haven't answered the small boy's question, but I can echo the question which St Paul asked when writing to his friends in Rome: 'Who shall separate us from the love of Christ? Shall tribulation, or distress, or persecution, or famine, or nakedness, or peril, or sword?' . . . And then Paul gives the triumphant answer, which he knows is absolutely true: '*No*. In all these things we are more than conquerors through him who loved us. For I am sure that neither death nor life, nor principalities, nor things present, nor things to come, nor height, nor depth, nor powers, nor anything else in all creation, will be able to separate us from the love of God in Christ Jesus our Lord.'

The Psalmist, David, could cry out to God in his troubles – and he had his share of them – and often complained to God, and questioned him. Yet he knew that wherever he went, however low he sank or high he rose, this fact was sure: 'even there your hand shall lead me, and your right hand shall hold me.'

God's hand is upon us and for us – you and me. If we will put our lives into his hands, we can know his support and his guidance every day of our lives.

Thank you, Lord, for the helping hands I have experienced in my life; the hands that brought me into the world, cared for me, encouraged me, trained me. Thank you for those who have given me a hand this week. Thank you for my hands. Show me how to use them to help, and not to hinder, the lives of others, for Christ's sake. Amen.

Right on time

There is a modern hymn which is a great favourite of mine –
'Tell out, my soul, the greatness of the Lord.' It has really
caught on over the last few years, and not surprisingly. It's
very singable. It has what I call 'guts' – it is cheerful, strong
and confident. It is based on the Magnificat, the Song of
Mary recorded in the first chapter of St Luke's Gospel, which
is said or sung daily in the Anglican service of Evening
Prayer.

I enjoy both the traditional version, sung as a chant, and
the modern hymn version, and I always sing them with great
gusto. But I have to remind myself of what the words are all
about, for they are the response of Mary to the news that she
was to become the mother of the Son of God.

At the time, Mary wasn't married; she was just a young
girl, engaged to a man named Joseph. It was a rather
frightening position to find herself in – young, unmarried
and pregnant. Who would believe her story about an angel
messenger? Yet she accepted that this was the will of God, his
purpose for her life; and she rejoiced that God had chosen her
to be the mother of the Messiah. Would any of us have sung
the words so heartily if we had been in Mary's position?

There have been occasions in my life when I have thought
God has had a strange sense of timing, when things have
seemed to happen at quite the wrong time for me, or what I
hoped would happen didn't materialise. Yet, as I look back, I
can see that in fact his timing was just right; it was mine that
was way out. It is easy, perhaps, to sing the Magnificat
looking back; not so easy to trust God for the future and sing,
and mean, 'My soul does magnify the Lord.'

Mary accepted God's timing, for she realised that all of time belongs to God, and that he uses it in his own way. I often find that quite hard to understand and to accept, don't you? But I remember reading some words a few years ago: 'Every moment of life is free time.' At that time I was so busy, I just laughed. Free time! Mine was completely tied up. And then the truth sank in. Every moment is free; it is God's gift to us, freely given to us to share. This is the real currency of life, more precious than pounds, dollars, or the most superior credit card.

Mary accepted that God's timing was perfect, even though she may not have understood it completely. And when we, too, come to realise that in our lives, then maybe we will stop getting so worked up about things, dashing here, there and everywhere, and begin to live life a day at a time – thanking God for his time, sharing it with others, enjoying it, and really making the most of it.

There is a book in the Old Testament called Ecclesiastes. It means 'the Preacher', and like most preachers the writer goes on a bit, asking questions, and then trying to give the answers. He says that there is a time for everything in life, both good and bad: 'For everything there is a season, and a time for every matter under heaven.' And when he has listed a whole load of happenings, which are all part and parcel of life, he says: 'I have seen the business that God has given to the sons of men to be busy with. He has made everything beautiful in its time. Also he has put eternity into man's mind.' Everything in its own time – giving us plenty to do, to enjoy, to work at; but also giving us another perspective on life, a sense of the eternal.

I suppose what the Preacher is saying is that we should take a day at a time, the rough and the smooth, and trust God to share it with us and get us through. I reckon our problem is doing just that. We tend either to look back over our shoulder, saying, 'If only I could have my time over again,' or else to try to sort out tomorrow, panicking about it and getting depressed. And so we work ourselves up into a state and fail to live the day we've got. We lose out on today because of yesterday's mistakes or the fear of tomorrow. That is human nature.

People don't change, and Jesus was speaking to folk just like us when he preached the Sermon on the Mount, as we call it. He was talking to worriers, people wrapped up in fear and anxiety, wondering how to get through all their problems – people just like us.

> *Therefore I tell you, do not be anxious about your life, what you shall eat or what you shall drink, nor about your body, what you shall put on. Is not life more than food, and the body more than clothing? Look at the birds of the air; they neither sow nor reap nor gather into barns, and yet your heavenly Father feeds them. Are you not of more value than they? And which of you by being anxious can add one cubit to his span of life? And why are you anxious about clothing? Consider the lilies of the field, how they grow; they neither toil nor spin; yet I tell you, even Solomon in all his glory was not arrayed like one of these. But if God so clothes the grass of the field, which today is alive and tomorrow is thrown into the oven, will he not much more clothe you, O men of little faith?*
>
> *Therefore do not be anxious, saying, 'What shall we eat?' or 'What shall we drink?' or 'What shall we wear?' For the Gentiles seek all these things; and your heavenly Father knows that you need them all. But seek first his kingdom and his righteousness, and all these things shall be yours as well.*

Take life a day at a time. It's the only way, isn't it? And the good news is that, as Christians, we not only have someone with us day by day in time, but for all eternity.

I see eternity as endless, day after day, but timeless. I've sometimes had a taste of eternity when seeing something breathtakingly beautiful, hearing marvellous music, being in good company – even, dare I say it, having a good laugh! It has been sheer joy. Time has not mattered. It has all been absolute delight. It has been as if time has stood still.

I believe that is what eternity – heaven – is like, for ever. I believe God gives us glimpses of heaven to encourage us, almost as though he draws back the curtain and allows us to peep through. St John writes of this in the book of Revelation: 'After this I looked, and lo, I saw in heaven an open door . . .'

I, too, need that open door experience to keep me going, for it makes all the difference to my day-by-day attitude to life. We all need a sense of the eternal, a vision of the end of time – in the best possible way. Eternity is to be enjoyed, not endured, that's for sure.

Thank you, Lord, for this day, with its demands, its opportunities, its pleasures. Help us to remember that, whatever it brings, you share it with us, and will bring us through it. Thank you, too, for the promise of eternity, of timeless enjoyment. May we begin to experience it here and now. And so, into your loving hands we commend ourselves, our families and friends, all those who share our days, both now and for ever more. Amen.

God's top ten

I don't like being told what to do and what not to do. I'm over twenty-one, and I reckon I can decide for myself. After all, it's my life, and if I choose to make a mess of it, that's up to me.

The trouble is, that what I do, or don't do, doesn't only affect me. It affects other people – my family, the folk I work with, the people I bump into. It's a sort of chain reaction; and if I'm going in the wrong direction, I can cause quite a snarl-up, and other people besides me can get hurt.

The ten commandments are very definite on Do's and Don'ts. There's no beating about the bush with them. But why bother about them? I suppose the difference between them and other Do's and Don'ts is that they are God's instructions. So maybe we do need to take heed of what they say. After all, God is our maker, and it could be that following the maker's instructions could save us a lot of trouble.

Perhaps the first thing to do is to find out what they are, and see if they have anything to say to us. After all, it is a long time since they were first set down, and they may have no bearing on our lives. On the other hand . . .

1

I am the Lord your God who brought you out of Eygpt, where you were slaves. Worship no God but me.

Well, that doesn't apply to me. I've never been to Egypt, I'm nobody's slave, and I'm Church of England. But I get the point. I think what it is saying is that God *has* had to rescue me. Because we are all slaves to one thing or another – to

93

time, to habits, to people. It is often like a treadmill; we can't get off. And, in a way, these things become like gods. We put them first in our lives, we have to put all our effort into satisfying them, and God has to take his turn for our attention. An hour on Sunday if he is lucky, the odd prayer when we are a bit desperate, but otherwise – well, he is way back in the queue.

I remember how, when I was at school, I used to get in a mess with maths. I wanted to do other, more exciting, things, and the teacher used to say, 'First things first, Margaret.' She was right, of course. If only I had got my priorities right, settled down and stuck at the maths, then other things would have fallen into place. And, I suppose, if I put God first, at the top of my priority list, then life might fall into place a bit more.

Well, it's never too late to try, is it?

2

Have you got any graven images around? The second of the ten commandments says, *You shall not make for yourself any graven image.* But I don't suppose many of us go round carving up wood and stone, or moulding images out of bits of plastic or clay; because they can't do anything for us – they are only things. Though, come to think of it, I suppose things can be worshipped – like that piece of metal outside called a car, the box in the corner of the room which demands so much attention, or the computer in the spare bedroom which keeps me glued to it, regardless of what else needs to be done.

I may not have made these things personally, but I'm quite hooked on them. I do give them far too much of my time, and I do expect them to give me satisfaction beyond what they are able – after all, they are only things.

Things can take over our lives. We don't always notice it happening, though. Take a look at the things in your life. Could it be they are 'graven images'?

It's a bit pointless worshipping them, isn't it? Much more

sensible to give the worship to someone who is worth it, someone who can give real satisfaction. Like God.

3

Swearing seems to have got far more sophisticated than when I was a kid. Some words I hear today, I'd never heard up to a few years ago, but they leave me in no doubt what they mean. There is something different about the sound of swear words. I suppose that's why children pick them up so easily, and find them so exciting.

I remember, when I was about eight, my mother telling me that if I swore, God would strike me dead. After a while I became so curious I tried one out, and was quite disappointed that there was no bolt from the blue. It was rather a let down.

The third commandment says, *You shall not take the name of the Lord your God in vain*; you shall not use God's name as a swear word. And yet 'God' and 'Jesus Christ' are among the most usual swear words. I don't suppose most people give much thought to it – they are just words. But then, do we pay enough attention to the words we use? Speech can be so beautiful. It is a pity to debase lovely words.

Words express how we feel. The eyes may be the window of the soul, but what comes out of the mouth reveals what we are. I read somewhere that God gave us two ears and one mouth, to be used in that proportion. Maybe if we stopped and listened to ourselves talking sometimes, we would get a shock.

The old war time slogan said, 'Careless talk costs lives.' The wrong use of words can mar our lives – and others'. So watch what you say today.

4

What do you do on Sundays? I suppose it depends on your job; lots of people have to work shifts – we would be in a mess if they didn't. They don't have a choice. But most of us do have a choice, and for many, I suppose, it is a 'lie-in' that we choose – after all, Sunday is a day of rest . . .

But that is not quite what the fourth commandment says. It is often misquoted. What it actually says is, *Remember the Sabbath day to keep it holy.* And that means far more than having a lie-in, taking the dog for a walk, or cleaning the car. Keeping it holy means making it special by worshipping God; giving him time and attention, instead of ourselves.

I find that going to church on Sundays, joining in worship with others, centring my thoughts on God, is so relaxing. It enables me to get the rest of the week into perspective, to see beyond myself and my own ideas, to get a vision of eternal values. It provides me with recreation, so that the next six days make sense. And that can't be bad, can it?

Try it for yourself next Sunday, and feel the difference.

5

I watched them out of the corner of my eye; they were shuffling impatiently, and as I turned to look at them the man at the front glanced at his watch, then caught my eye and looked away sheepishly. They were in a hurry, and I was delaying them. They wanted me to get a move on. I was taking dad's funeral.

Yes, it was understandable. Their father had been a tartar, he had lived to be eighty-six, and they were going off on their holidays immediately the service was over. But it was sad that they begrudged him this last half hour. They were not prepared to give him that respect.

Honour your father and your mother is the first of the commandments dealing with our relationship with other people – and it is not there by accident. Our attitude to our parents is vitally important. It colours all our family relationships.

It is said that 'God gives us our relations, but we can choose our friends.' True. But do you see your relations as God's gifts? Your mother and father as an honour? An old lady was telling me recently about her son. He had done very well in life, and had got on in his chosen career, but he never came to see her now. He didn't even write, only at Christmas. 'I reckon he's too busy,' she said sadly, and then she added, 'But he will be old one day. What then . . .?'

What then, indeed.

6

Open your daily paper, and I guarantee it will contain some reports of murders. There will be massacres, the result of war and conflict; premeditated murders; so-called 'crimes of passion', committed in hot blood; and there will be accidental murders, the result of anger, fear or jealousy getting out of hand. We read about them and say, 'What is the world coming to?'

How many murders have you committed? None? Well, have you ever said to somebody 'You fool'; or 'I could murder him'? Oh, we don't mean it – or do we? The anger rises, and we lash out with our tongue and say cutting things. Jesus said that if we are angry like that, it is just the same as killing people – committing murder.

The violence in the world is not caused by governments, or by the generals, or by political situations going wrong; but by folk like you and me seeing other people as of less value than ourselves, as inconveniences, as obstacles to what we want. So we push them aside and discard them – and something in them dies, and we have caused it.

There is enough trouble in the world without us making it. How much better to bring a bit of life into today for someone else. *You shall do no murder*.

7

One in three marriages finishes up in the divorce courts, so we are told. And if you add to them those married people who are carrying on with someone else, the percentage of broken marriages is frightening. Over and over again, I have been saddened by the news of yet another broken marriage caused by a third party – what is known as an 'adulterous relationship'.

The commandment is *You shall not commit adultery*. But where does adultery start? A casual meeting, a glance exchanged, a night out, a 'working late at the office', a wife bored with the house and kids – and before you know it, it is quite out of hand, and you are unable to stop it.

Jesus said that if you look at someone lustfully, you have already committed adultery in your heart – no exaggeration, when you come to think about it. For that is where it starts, in the heart; in the looking; in the desiring. It does start in a small way, and it is better to stop it before it gets out of hand. We are all human, and we like to have what takes our fancy. But if he or she belongs to someone else, stop. Before it is too late, before the damage is done, and lives and happiness are ruined.

8

It is over twenty years now since the Great Train Robbery. Somehow it captured the imagination of the public and the robbers became folk heroes. I wonder why. I suppose it was the bravado of the crime, the organisation of such a gigantic robbery, which made us draw our breath. Most of us have to admit to a bit of admiration for their dash and style.

I read the other day of a robbery at an old lady's home. She had only a few pounds in the house, yet the thieves frightened the old lady almost to death, knocked her about, messed up the house, and now she is scared to live there any more. And that fills us all with revulsion for such a crime.

I don't suppose we are likely to attempt a great train robbery, or to bash an old lady for a few pounds. But have you ever got off the bus without paying? Made personal calls on your boss's phone? Put a few screws in your pocket to do a job at home? Left work half an hour early? Or doctored your Income Tax return?

It's all stealing, whether from an organisation, a company,

98

or an individual. Stealing is stealing, is stealing – but of course, 'everybody does it'. That is no excuse in the eyes of the law, or in the eyes of God. The commandment is *You shall not steal*; and 'you' means you, and me. It is easy to point the finger at someone else; we all need to keep our own houses in order, and respect what belongs to other people. After all, we wouldn't want it to happen to us, would we?

9

'I swear to tell the truth, the whole truth, and nothing but the truth' – words well known, whether from real life experience or from watching soap opera court dramas on television.

Do you tell the truth, the whole truth, and nothing but the truth? If you do, you are pretty unique. We may not be blatant liars, but how often do we, by leaving out something, distort the truth; or by adding our ideas or thoughts paint an entirely different picture from the real one? We don't even have to open our mouths to 'bear false witness'; we all project an image of ourselves to the world at large, and does it really bear any resemblance to the real us? What lies behind the smile, the nod, the handshake? When we sign a letter 'yours sincerely', are we really?

Truth is a very strange and elusive commodity. No wonder Pilate said, with a sneer, to Jesus, 'What is truth?' Perhaps our own experience of life leads us to say those same words. We have been let down plenty of times ourselves.

Do not bear false witness. To be honest and open is very dangerous. We can get hurt, be let down, be laughed at. But what matters in the end is truth, and you can't put a price on that, can you?

10

We hadn't got much money when we were first married. It took us all our time to keep our heads above water, and pay the mortgage on our small semi which backed on to the railway line.

One day I found a handbag, bulging with cash, cheque book, credit cards – the lot. It had the owner's address in it, so we phoned up and went to return it straight away. The owner was very grateful, and gave us afternoon tea, and we enjoyed meeting her. Her house was like something out of *Homes and Gardens*, large, with elegant furnishings, and a garden which swept down to open countryside. It was absolutely beautiful, and very expensive – but obviously they could afford it.

How I envied that house and life style! When I looked at our semi and the view over the railway line, I hated what we had. I'd seen what I really wanted, and it bore no resemblance to what we had got. I felt like that for quite a while. I began to get bitter and twisted and discontented inside. I made myself miserable. Then one day I looked at my home and family and realised just how lucky I was – and the desire for the other place faded.

The tenth commandment is a wise one: *Do not covet*. It is for our protection, for we fail to appreciate what we have when we strain after what the other person has. Like the old hymn says:

Count your blessings, name them one by one,
And it will surprise you what the Lord has done.

* * *

It is not often that we hear the ten commandments read out in church these days. It tends just to be the summary: 'Love God, and love your neighbour.' And that is a pity, because we can kid ourselves we love God and our neighbour, for we interpret love as not doing them any harm. And it is not until we read or hear the ten commandments that we realise that there is a lot more to them than that. They are very personal and direct, and are not about our rights, but about our responsibilities; not vague ideas, but definite commands.

'If everybody lived by the ten commandments the world

would be a better place.' That is often said – and it's true, isn't it? But in place of 'everybody', put 'I', and try by God's grace to live by them. I think we shall find that not only will the world, our bit of the world, be a better place, but we will become better people, and a bit more like the person we really want to be – free to be ourselves.

Of course, we can't do it on our own. But God doesn't intend we shall. He offers us his help, his strength. We have to provide the will.

Why not have a go?

Meditation on the Lord's Prayer

A new day. What does it hold for me?
I need someone to hold on to.
I need someone to trust, someone who won't let me down.
Someone bigger than me, better than me,
Someone I can love and respect,
Someone I can talk to right now.
Our Father, who art in heaven,
    hallowed be your name.
Thank you for being my Father!

What a frightening world I live in.
An angry world – a sad world.
A violent world – an unfair world.
Why can't it be
A loving world – a happy world?
A peaceful world – a sharing world?
Why is it so often hell when it should be heaven?
Your kingdom come.
Father, help me today to do something towards
    making this world more like you intend it to be,
by your rule of love.

What does God want to do with me?
What does God want me to do for him?
What does God want me to do for others?
If I say yes, it may cost me everything.
It may not be the way I wanted to go.
It may not be easy if I pray
Your will be done, on earth as it is in heaven.
Dare I pray it, and mean it?
Father, help me to do your will,
this day and every day.

How am I going to manage tomorrow
   if the cheque doesn't arrive?
What about the bills at the end of the month?
How can I afford the insurance premium
   due at the end of the year?
What should I pray for?
Give us this day our daily bread.
Father, help me to trust you for today,
and leave tomorrow in your hands.

I'll never forgive them for what they did to me.
They were so rude, so mean, so unkind.
They deceived me and hurt me,
they let me down.
I will never forget.
I never hurt anyone –
only when they provoke me,
or when I'm tired, or it's a mistake,
or when I'm not thinking . . .
and I do ask for forgiveness from God.
Forgive us our debts, as we also
   have forgiven our debtors.
Father, help me to forgive and forget
and know the joy of forgiveness this day.

Why are wrong things so attractive?
They look so good, feel so good.
They offer me pleasure and delight.
Surely it wouldn't matter if
   it was just this once,
if I tried just a little . . .
I could always stop when I wanted to.
Lead us not into temptation,
But deliver us from evil.
Father,
Keep me under your protection this day.
Give me the will to say no to sin,
and yes to you.

103

Why does power always seem to bring out
   the worst in people?
The empire builders, the glory seekers,
They seem to have taken over the world.
They treat everybody as though they own them.
No wonder there is so much trouble in the world,
all the power struggles, political take-overs,
the riots and revolutions.
Father, help me to remember that you are
Lord God Almighty, and that
Yours is the kingdom,
the power and the glory,
now and for ever and ever.
And remind me of that glorious fact every day. Amen

MARGARET CUNDIFF

What reviewers have said about her books

Her light touch is a tonic . . . humour and resourcefulness, candour
and warmth, vigour and the relish of life.
C of E Newspaper

Realistic and hilarious.
Christian Bookseller

Peppered with humour . . . rich in commitment.
Yorkshire Evening Post

Will dismiss many doubts about the contribution women can make
to the Christian ministry.
Radio Sheffield

For her, the greatest sin is to make Jesus dull.
C of E Newspaper

(*Living by the Book*) makes the Sermon on the Mount spring into the
life and thought world of the twentieth century. She has this
astonishing knack of clothing the heart of the message
in today's dress.
Michael Green in the *Church Times*

Margaret Cundiff has no illusions about human nature. She portrays
herself and her fellow human beings as they are and then uses Jesus'
teaching to challenge them to live as they *could*, with his help.
Floodtide

More Christian paperbacks from

Tri∧ngle

David Adam
THE EDGE OF GLORY
Modern prayers in the Celtic tradition

THE CRY OF THE DEER
Meditations on the Hymn of St Patrick

Ralph Capenerhurst
CLOCKING IN
Reminiscences of a shop steward turned industrial chaplain

Frank Pagden
LOOKING SIDEWAYS AT GOD
A simple introduction to belief, for beginners and non-churchgoers

Frances Parsons
POOLS OF FRESH WATER
A personal story of healing and the beginning of a healing ministry

Edith Schaeffer
FOREVER MUSIC: *A tribute to the gift of creativity*
Reflections on music, creativity and marriage

Derek Williams (Editor)
TIME TO LIVE
Eight people from different walks of life write about how they
manage their time

For a complete list of Triangle publications write to: Triangle/SPCK,
Holy Trinity Church, Marylebone Road, London NW1 4DU